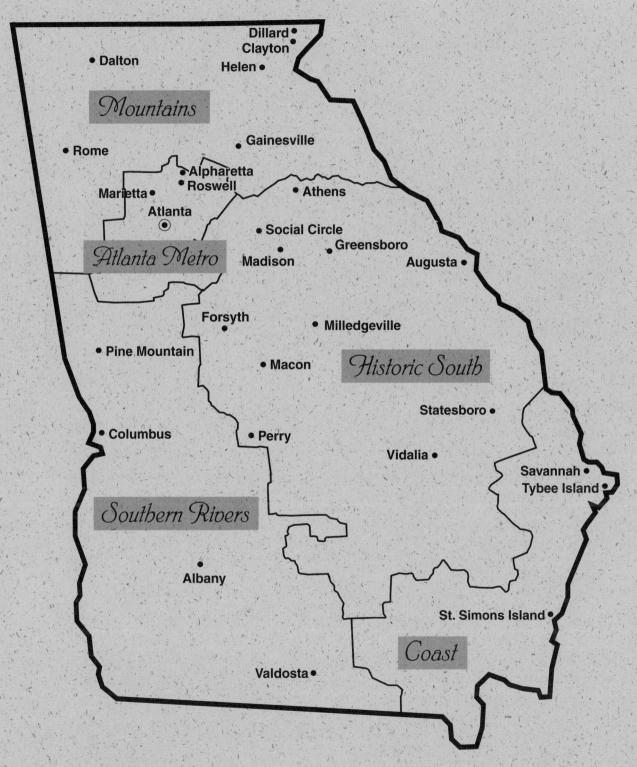

Dillard •
Clayton •
• Dalton
Helen •

Mountains

• Rome
• Gainesville
• Alpharetta
• Roswell
• Athens
Marietta •
Atlanta
◉
• Social Circle
Atlanta Metro
Madison •
• Greensboro
Augusta •

Forsyth •
• Milledgeville
• Pine Mountain
• Macon
Historic South
Statesboro •
• Columbus
• Perry
Vidalia •
Southern Rivers
Savannah •
Tybee Island •

• Albany
St. Simons Island •

Coast
Valdosta •

Five Regions of Georgia with towns noted
where restaurants are located.

Fine Dining Georgia Style

Signature Recipes from Georgia's Restaurants and Bed & Breakfast Inns

Fine Dining
Georgia Style

Signature Recipes from Georgia's
Restaurants and Bed & Breakfast Inns

by John M. Bailey

QUAIL RIDGE PRESS
Preserving America's Food Heritage

Library of Congress Cataloging-in-Publication Data

Bailey, John M.. 1936-
    Fine dining Georgia style : signature recipes from Georgia's restaurants and
bed & breakfast inns / John M. Bailey
        p. cm.
    ISBN 1-893062-66-X
        1. Cookery, American—Southern Style. 2. Cookery—Georgia. 3. Restaurants—
    Georgia I. Title.

TX715.2.S68B33 2004
    641.5975—dc22   2004024434

ISBN 1-893062-66-X

Front cover photo of Callaway Gardens, Pine Mountain, Georgia, by John Bailey.
Design by Cynthia Clark.
Pen and ink drawings by Gary Gibson and Bill Williams © Levee Group Corporation.
Pen and ink drawings of The Coast Region by Pam Lee, artist.
Manufactured in the United States of America.

QUAIL RIDGE PRESS
P. O. Box 123 • Brandon, MS 39043 • 1-800-343-1583
email: info@quailridge.com • www.quailridge.com

Dedication

*This book is dedicated to my wonderful wife Ann
for her continued love and support for my projects.*

Table of Contents

Introduction

$\mathcal{T}$his is the fourth in a series of state-specific cookbooks to showcase the many fine chefs and restaurants in the South. Let this book be your guide to talented chefs and great restaurants across the state of Georgia. As expected, the food was wonderful and the chefs were anxious to share their signature recipes for this project. Because of space availability, we were unable to use recipes from all of the fine dining restaurants in the state. If we missed a couple of your favorite restaurants, please forgive us. We are, however, extremely pleased with the recipes that we have, and think that these recipes represent a good sampling of the fine food that is available across the state of Georgia.

The Georgia Department of Tourism has divided the state into five distinctly different and beautiful areas: the Mountains Region, the Atlanta Metro Region, the Historic South Region, the Coast Region, and the Southern Rivers Region. I used this as a guideline when I visited the state. The state is certainly blessed to have such beautiful scenery, friendly people, and wonderful food! Even though most of the recipes are fine dining recipes, we have also included recipes from other popular Georgia restaurants known for southern cooking. These recipes have been tested over the years in restaurants and inns throughout Georgia. Now you can enjoy them in your home. They are on the house, compliments of the chef!

John M. Bailey

Acknowledgments

I would like to thank the following people:

The chefs of Georgia for all of their great recipes

The local chapters of the Georgia Chamber of Commerce for their help

Pam Lee, artist, and Gary Gibson and Bill Williams, for the use of their beautiful pen and ink drawings

Lauren Yawn, the director of Statesboro Convention & Visitors Bureau
for her assistance during the development process

Stacie Hanna with the Buckhead Life Group for her assistance

Georgia Department of Tourism for descriptive information

Special thanks to Rachel Crumbley at Callaway Gardens for all her help on this project

My grandson, John M. Bailey III, for assisting me with the photography

W. Jett Wilson, attorney and Ed Neal, CPA for their help with this project

John T. Edge, Georgia native and Director of the Southern Foodways Alliance
at the University of Mississippi, for restaurant and Georgia history information

JMB

About the Author

John Bailey, author of *Fine Dining Mississippi Style*, *Fine Dining Tennessee Style*, and *Fine Dining Louisiana Style*, is a graduate of the University of Mississippi. He is a member of the Southern Foodways Alliance and a frequent judge at many culinary events. In his spare time, John enjoys photography, cooking, and collecting cookbooks. A native of Mississippi, he and his wife Ann reside in Germantown, Tennessee.

The Mountains Region

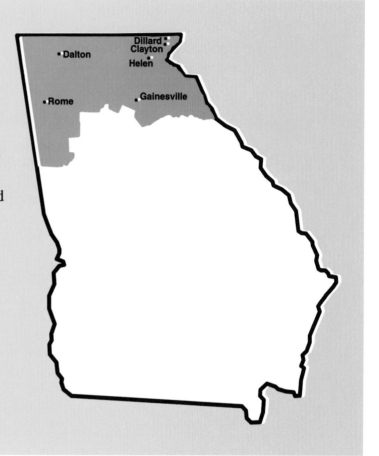

Stunning mountains, glistening lakes, and raging rivers make up the dramatic Mountains Region. While in Rome visit one of the South's largest Victorian districts. If you are more interested in outdoor sports, head to Gainesville where location is everything. Nestled in the foothills of the Blue Ridge Mountains and bordered by the shores of Lake Sidney Lanier, Gainesville is popular for both motor and water sports. Celebrate gold rush days every October in Dahlonega, the site of the first major U.S. gold rush. Then travel to the small Appalachian town of Helen for the annual Bavarian Oktoberfest celebration. There's something for everyone in the mountains of Georgia.

The Mountains Region Menu

(*continued*)

The Mountains Region Menu

NACOOCHEE GRILL *(Helen)*
Nacoochee Valley Crab Cakes
   with Red Pepper Coulis...18
Crème Brûlée...19
Veal Meatloaf 19

COUNTRY GENTLEMAN RESTAURANT *(Rome)*
Greek Village Salad...20
Penne, Sausage, and Broccoli 20
Fettuccini Alfredo 20
Veal Scaloppine..20

Pazzo Pizzeria & Italian Market

5136 Laurel Lodge Road
Clayton, GA 30525
(706) 947-0408

"A Little Piece of Italy at Lake Burton"

Big Bite Catering features a combined 60 years of food and beverage experience through restaurateurs Gene Marra (owner/chef), James Gill (manager of Pazzo/catering division), and Amanda Granberry (chef of Pazzo/off-property catering).

Taramasalata

$\frac{1}{3}$ loaf French bread, crust removed	10 ounces tarama (carp roe)
$\frac{1}{2}$ cup cold water	2 tablespoons chopped parsley, preferably fresh
1 medium white onion, cut and quartered	$2\frac{1}{2}$ to 3 cups olive oil, divided
2 cloves garlic	1 lemon, juiced
$\frac{1}{2}$ teaspoon cumin	
1 teaspoon oregano	

Soak bread until soggy. Squeeze out excess water until barely moist. In food processor, chop onion and garlic until fine. Add herbs, tarama, parsley, bread, and 1 cup oil. Blend together until smooth. While still blending, add remaining oil slowly until completely incorporated. Add lemon juice. The Taramasalata should thicken to heavy mayonnaise. If necessary, add water to thin. Refrigerate several hours before serving. Spread on toast points to serve.

Pazzo Chicken

4 chicken breasts, quartered, bone-in with skin	$\frac{1}{2}$ cup kalamata olives
Salt and pepper to taste	$\frac{1}{2}$ cup chopped artichoke hearts
4 Italian link sausages, sliced	$\frac{1}{3}$ cup rehydrated and julienned sun-dried tomatoes
6 parboiled baby red potatoes, quartered	8 whole pepperoncini peppers
$\frac{1}{2}$ cup olive oil	3 lemons, juiced
3 tablespoons fresh rosemary	$1\frac{1}{2}$ cups good white wine
$\frac{1}{4}$ cup finely chopped parsley	3 tablespoons basil chiffonade
$1\frac{1}{2}$ tablespoon dried oregano	

Preheat convection oven to 425°. Season chicken lightly with salt and pepper. In a roasting pan, toss together chicken, sausage, potatoes, olive oil, and all of the herbs except basil. Place in oven and cook for 10 to 15 minutes until lightly browned. Reduce heat to 325°. Add remaining ingredients, except for basil. Cook until chicken reaches 180° with a meat thermometer. Remove and finish with fresh basil. Serves 8.

Mascarpone with Fresh Berries

16 ounces mascarpone	1 teaspoon salt
4 egg yolks	$\frac{1}{2}$ cup hazelnut liqueur
$\frac{3}{4}$ cup heavy cream	2 cups fresh strawberries, raspberries, or blueberries
1 tablespoon vanilla extract	
Juice of half a lemon	4 biscotti cookies
$\frac{1}{2}$ cup confectioners' sugar	Whipped cream

Put mascarpone into a food processor, with the processor running. Add egg yolks, cream, vanilla, lemon juice, powdered sugar and salt. Lastly, add hazelnut liqueur. Blend until slightly thicker than heavy cream, but do not overmix or ingredients will separate. Chill for 2 hours. Pour over fresh berries. Garnish with biscotti and whipped cream. Serves 4.

The Cellar Restaurant

1331 W Walnut Avenue
Dalton, GA 30720
(706) 226-6029

Linda Fricks, Owner

Grilled Swordfish Perfumed with Preserved Lemons

PRESERVED LEMONS:

10 lemons	10 black peppercorns
2 tablespoons kosher salt, divided	4 bay leaves
	½ cup olive oil
6 garlic cloves	Juice of 10 to 12 lemons

Quarter each lemon from the top to within ¾ inch from the bottom so the quarters remain intact. Sprinkle 1 tablespoon salt across the cut lemons and put the remaining 1 tablespoon salt in the bottom of a large pickling jar. Pack the lemons in the jar, pushing them down as much as possible along with the garlic, peppercorns, and bay leaves.

Add the oil and enough lemon juice to cover the lemons and seal the jar. Store at room temperature for a minimum of 3 weeks before using. Shake the jar every other day to redistribute ingredients.

Lemons must be immersed in salt, oil, and lemon juice at all times. Before using, rinse the lemons and discard the meat. Preserved lemons will keep for up to 2 years.

TRUFFLE MASHED POTATOES:

1 cup celery root, cooked to fork-tender	1/2 cup heavy cream
	Salt and ground black pepper to taste
1 pound Idaho potatoes, washed, peeled, and cubed	Truffle oil
5 tablespoons unsalted butter	

(continued)

(Grilled Swordfish continued)

In a medium saucepan, place the potatoes in enough water to cover; bring to a boil. Reduce heat and cook until tender, about 20 to 25 minutes. Drain well and place in mixing bowl. Add remaining ingredients except truffle oil, and beat until smooth, using a mixer. Transfer potatoes to a serving bowl and drizzle with truffle oil.

4 (6-ounce) swordfish fillets	Potato chips, crushed
	Truffle oil
Salt and ground black pepper to taste	Preserved Lemons

Rub fillets with skin of preserved lemons. Season each fillet with salt and pepper and grill for 3 minutes on each side or until cooked through.

When ready to serve, place Truffle Mashed Potatoes in center of each serving plate. Place one fillet on top of each serving of potatoes and garnish with crushed potato chips. Drizzle with truffle oil on the side of each plate as a garnish. Serves 4.

Caesar Salad

4 cups mayonnaise	1 tablespoon black pepper
1¼ cups sour cream	½ tablespoon Worcestershire sauce
1 egg, uncooked	
2 tablespoons diced celery	6 cups chopped romaine lettuce
1 tablespoon diced anchovies	2 tablespoons Parmesan cheese
1 large onion, diced	
2 tablespoons freshly minced garlic	Croutons

In a medium bowl, combine all ingredients except lettuce, cheese, and croutons. Mix well and chill for 15 minutes. In a large bowl, toss dressing with lettuce; top with croutons and sprinkle with Parmesan cheese. Serves 6.

Crème Brûlée

3 cups whipping cream	**11 egg yolks**
1 vanilla bean, split	**⅓ cup sugar**
lengthwise	

Pour cream into a medium saucepan. Scrape the seeds from inside of vanilla bean into cream, then add the bean. Bring cream to a simmer and remove from heat. Discard vanilla bean.

In a large bowl, whisk egg yolks and sugar. Gradually whisk eggs and sugar into hot mixture over medium-low heat, stirring constantly, but do not boil. Cook about 2 minutes or until liquid coats the spoon. Pour liquid through a fine strainer into custard cups.

Preheat oven to 350°. Arrange the cups in a large baking pan. Add enough hot water to the pan to come halfway up the sides of the custard cups. Bake for 30 to 40 minutes or until custard is softly set. Move cups to a wire rack and cool. Chill at least 3 hours.

Just before serving, sprinkle tops of each custard with brown sugar and broil for 2 minutes or until golden brown. Chill again before serving. Serves 4 to 6.

Wink Theatre, Dalton

The Dillard House

U.S. Highway 441
Dillard, GA 30537
(800) 541-0671
www.dillardhouse.com

The restaurant was founded in 1917 by Carrie E. Dillard who started an inn and restaurant. *Southern Living's* Reader Choice Award has been given for eight consecutive years as Best Southern Cooking Restaurant.

Our facilities offer everything the frequent traveler has come to expect. All of our guest rooms are new or newly renovated. Charming suites and cottages are also available. You also have the option of staying in a secluded, intimate mountainside chalet. Whatever the season, beauty abounds at the Dillard House. In Spring you will be treated to acres of gardens in full bloom with tulips, rhododendron and mountain laurel. Summer offers a feast of flowers including impatiens, geraniums, dahlia, roses, hydrangea and salvia. Wildflowers bloom in all seasons. Autumn in the mountains is breathtaking. Colorful foliage abounds at the Dillard House. Winter is serene and offers some wonderful views since there are no leaves to obstruct your vision. And don't forget the snow! Nothing is quite as tranquil as looking out over a snow covered valley and mountain range.

The following recipes are from *The Dillard House Cookbook.*

Butternut Squash Soufflé

2 large butternut squash, peeled, seeded, cooked, and drained	½ teaspoon ground ginger
1 cup sugar	4 eggs, beaten
	1 teaspoon vanilla

Mash cooked butternut squash, or put them into a mixing bowl and beat at medium speed. Mix squash, sugar, ginger, eggs, and vanilla. Pour into a buttered 2-quart casserole dish. Prepare Topping.

TOPPING:

½ cup brown sugar	¼ cup chopped pecans
½ cup flour	¼ cup flaked coconut
¼ stick margarine, melted	(optional)

Mix all ingredients and spread over squash. Bake in a preheated oven at 325° for 30 to 40 minutes. (You can also top soufflé with just coconut, if desired.) Yields 6 servings.

Blackberry Cobbler

1 quart blackberries (fresh or frozen)	½ cup cornstarch
1 cup water	Melted butter for brushing pie pastry
½ to ⅔ cup sugar	
¼ cup butter or margarine	

Bring blackberries, water, sugar, and butter to a boil. Mix cornstarch with enough water to make a smooth paste. Stir paste into blackberries. Remove from heat and pour into an 8x10-inch baking dish. Top with pie pastry and brush with melted butter. Bake in a preheated oven at 350° for 30 minutes.

PASTRY:

⅔ cup shortening	6 tablespoons water or milk
2 cups self-rising flour	

Cut shortening into flour. Add liquid to form a stiff dough. Wrap in plastic wrap and chill in refrigerator for 1 hour. Roll out dough, and cut as desired to place on top of pie filling. Yields 6 to 8 servings.

Stuffed Cabbage

1 (2-pound) cabbage	1 egg
1 cup ground pork sausage, uncooked	½ teaspoon salt
1 cup bread crumbs	Chopped parsley or grated cheese to garnish

Cut cabbage halfway from top to base into 8 sections. Place cabbage into warm water for 10 minutes to soften leaves. Remove cabbage from water and carefully peel back 4 or 5 leaves of each section. Scoop out center of cabbage. Chop scooped-out leaves to yield 1 cup. Combine chopped cabbage, sausage, bread crumbs, egg, and salt and fill the cabbage cavity. Fold leaves over stuffing and cover with cheesecloth to hold folded leaves in place. Remove cheesecloth and place cabbage in casserole dish or pan. Add ½ cup water to pan. Cover and bake for 35 to 40 minutes at 325°. Garnish with chopped parsley or cheese. Serve with Basic White Sauce. Yields about 8 servings.

BASIC WHITE SAUCE:

1 cup margarine	Salt and pepper
3 tablespoons all-purpose flour	1 quart milk

Melt margarine in a saucepan and add flour, salt and pepper to make a paste. Add milk and cook until thick, stirring constantly. Yields 8 to 10 servings.

Bacon Roll-Ups

Bread slices	Onions
Cream cheese	Bacon, uncooked
Chives	

Remove crust from bread. Mix cream cheese, chives, and onions. Spread cream cheese mixture on bread. Cut bread in half. Take half of a slice of uncooked bacon and roll bread with bacon on the outside of the bread and the cream cheese on the inside of roll. Use a toothpick to secure the roll. Place roll-ups on cookie sheet and cook at 325° for 25 minutes. Turn roll-ups after cooking for half of the time. Serve warm.

Pumpkin Bread

5 cups all-purpose flour	4 teaspoons baking soda
4 cups sugar	2 teaspoons cinnamon
4 cups pumpkin	1 teaspoon salt
(butternut or banana	1 teaspoon vanilla
squash may be	1 cup chopped nuts
substituted)	Chopped dates or raisins
1 cup vegetable oil	(optional)
1 teaspoon ground cloves	

Mix all ingredients. Bake in 4 tall, 1-pound coffee cans. Fill about ½ to ⅔ full. Bake at 350° for 1 hour and 15 minutes. Bread will shake out of cans when cool. Plastic lids may be placed on cans for storage after cooling, if bread is left in cans. Store in refrigerator or freeze. Yields 12 to 14 servings.

Baked Ham

1 (10-pound) ham	Salt and pepper

Rub ham with salt and pepper. Cover with foil and bake at 350° until almost done, basting every 45 minutes with Honey Glaze. Bake ham uncovered for the last 40 minutes of cooking time.

HONEY GLAZE:

1/4 cup cornstarch	1/2 cup brown sugar
1 cup water	1 teaspoon dry mustard
1 quart pineapple juice	6 to 8 slices pineapple
1 quart honey	

Dissolve cornstarch in water. Bring juice, honey, sugar, and mustard to a gentle boil. Pour cornstarch into boiling mixture and stir until thickened.

To garnish, lay sliced pineapple on ham. Pour Honey Glaze over garnished ham and heat in 300° oven for 10 to 15 minutes. Yields 20 to 25 servings.

Cabbage Casserole

Lazell Vinson won first prize at the Dillard Cabbage Festival with this recipe.

1 large head cabbage	2 cups grated Cheddar
1 teaspoon salt	cheese
½ stick margarine	1½ cups buttered bread
3 cups Basic White Sauce	crumbs

Shred cabbage. Cook 5 to 8 minutes in boiling water with 1 teaspoon salt. Don't overcook; cabbage should remain crisp. Drain well. Layer in buttered 2-quart casserole the cabbage, enough Basic White Sauce to cover, second layer of cabbage, remaining sauce, then cheese. Top with buttered bread crumbs. Bake in preheated 300° oven for 15 to 20 minutes.

BASIC WHITE SAUCE:

3 tablespoons butter	Salt and pepper to taste
3 tablespoons all-purpose	3 cups milk
flour	

Melt margarine in sauce pot and add flour, salt and pepper to make a paste. Add milk and cook until thick, stirring constantly. Yields 8 to 10 servings.

Dillard House Fried Chicken

The Dillard House has cooked chicken this way for as long as any of the cooks can remember, and it remains a favorite with customers. Keys to the success of this recipe are the depth of grease in the frying pan, a heavy iron skillet, and double dipping the chicken in flour and buttermilk.

1 fresh 2-pound chicken	Salt and pepper to taste
Buttermilk	1½ cups shortening
3 cups all-purpose flour	
for dredging	

Cut chicken into quarters and wash. Put in a pan of buttermilk and soak for 15 to 20 minutes. Season the flour with salt and pepper. Dip chicken into flour. Dip back into the buttermilk and once again into the flour. Put the chicken into 1 inch shortening heated to 375° in a 12- to 14-inch heavy iron skillet. The chicken should not be crowded in the pan. Cook about 30 minutes, turning twice. Yields 4 servings.

Rudolph's on Green Street

700 Green Street
Gainesville, GA 30501
(770) 534-2226
www.rudolphsdining.com

Mr. and Mrs. Khawly, Owners
Michael Hunt, Executive Chef

Crab Cakes

3 eggs	4 ounces lemon juice
2 cups mayonnaise	2 ounces Lea & Perrin
4 ounces Dijon mustard	Worcestershire Sauce

Whisk it all together.

2¼ ounces bread crumbs per crab cake	Salt and fine black pepper to taste
½ ounce cracker crumbs per crab cake	½ cup chopped fresh parsley

Fold into liquid.

2 pounds jumbo lump crab	1 pound regular lump crab

Fold it into above mixture; shape and fry until done on medium setting. Yields 30 cakes with #16 scoop.

Banana Bread

4 bananas, chopped	2 tablespoons baking powder
⅔ cup shortening, melted	2½ teaspoons salt
2 eggs, beaten	⅔ cup sugar
2 cups milk	½ cup chopped walnuts
½ cup honey	½ cup chopped pecans
Squirt vanilla extract	
4 cups all-purpose flour	

Mix liquid (bananas, shortening, eggs, milk, honey, and vanilla extract) and add to sifted dry ingredients. Pour into greased pan. Bake at 350° for 1½ hours.

Nacoochee Grill

7277 South Main Street
Helen, GA 30545
(706) 878-8020
www.nacoocheegrill.com

Gene Marra, Owner/Chef

Crème Brûlée

1 quart heavy cream	½ tablespoon vanilla extract
1 whole egg	¼ teaspoon salt
9 egg yolks	5 ounces sugar to finish
½ cup sugar, for mix	

Preheat convection oven to 275° (conventional oven, 300°) In a saucepan on low heat, bring heavy cream to a low boil. Remove from heat. Combine whole egg, yolks, ½ cup sugar, vanilla, and salt in a mixing bowl and whisk thoroughly. With a ladle, temper hot cream into egg mixture, intermixing them gradually until combined. Whisk gently until all sugar is dissolved and mixture is smooth.

Pour into 5 (8-ounce) oven-safe ramekins in a bain marie, covered but well vented. Place in preheated oven and cook for 70 minutes. Uncover pan and shake it slightly. If you see any "loose spots" in centers of the crème brûlées, turn oven off and let them sit a few minutes longer with door closed. This should firm them up. Allow to cool at room temperature for about 15 minutes, then refrigerate for at least one hour.

Immediately before serving, evenly cover top of each chilled crème brûlée with one ounce of sugar. Place under a broiler, on the top rack on high heat, just long enough to caramelize the sugar. Remove from broiler and serve. Yields 5 (8-ounce) servings.

Nacoochee Valley Crab Cakes with Red Pepper Coulis

CRAB CAKES:

1 medium red bell pepper, finely chopped	2 whole eggs
1 bunch green onions, finely chopped	1 cup mayonnaise
	½ cup sour cream
1 Thai chile pepper, minced	4 teaspoons whole-grain mustard
2 tablespoons chopped parsley	4 teaspoons Worcestershire sauce
2 tablespoons Old Bay Seasoning	2½ cups crushed un-salted saltine crackers
	1 pound lump crabmeat

Combine all ingredients except crackers and crab-meat. Mix well. Add crackers and stir until they are absorbed by mixture. Gently fold in crabmeat until it is evenly dispersed, but do not overmix. For best results, chill at least 4 hours before using.

To cook crab cakes, preheat griddle to 325°. Scoop 4-ounce portions onto griddle. Brown on one side about 5 minutes, then flip over and press into patties. Cook an additional 5 minutes, or until brown. Serve hot with Red Pepper Coulis. Yields 2 (4-ounce) patties. Serves 8.

RED PEPPER COULIS:

2 cups heavy whipping cream	3 roasted red peppers, drained

Heat heavy cream and roasted peppers together in a small saucepan. Bring to a boil, then remove from heat. Purée mixture thoroughly and strain it to remove any solids. Keep warm.

Veal Meatloaf

½ cup Japanese bread crumbs	2 whole eggs
½ cup heavy cream	1 teaspoon minced garlic
2½ pounds ground veal	2 tablespoons Worcestershire sauce
½ bunch green onions, finely chopped	¼ cup chili powder
½ bunch cilantro, finely chopped	1 tablespoon traditional seasoned salt
1 cup shredded Cheddar cheese	1 tablespoon oregano
3 ounces finely chopped jalapeños	½ teaspoon coarse-ground black pepper

Preheat convection oven to 325° (or coventional oven to 350°) and grease a 2-quart loaf pan. Mix bread crumbs and cream together in a small dish; set aside. While this is setting, combine all other ingredients in a mixing bowl. Add bread crumb mixture and blend everything very thoroughly by hand. Press firmly into greased loaf pan, smoothing the top. Bake in preheated oven 45 minutes. Remove and cool at room temperature for 15 minutes before cutting. Serves 8 (6-ounce) portions.

Clock Tower, Rome

Country Gentleman Restaurant

26 Chateau Drive SE
Rome, GA 30161
(706) 295-0205

Greek Village Salad

½ medium head escarole
1 small head romaine
  lettuce
2 ripe tomatoes, cut into
  wedges
1 small cucumber, sliced
1 small pepper, sliced

1 small red onion, sliced
  into rings
½ pound feta cheese,
  crumbled
8 anchovy fillets
2 hard-boiled eggs, sliced

Tear crisp, cold salad greens into small pieces. Put into a large bowl, combine, and toss. Add remaining ingredients and Dressing and toss. Serves 4.

DRESSING:

¼ cup red wine vinegar
½ teaspoon salt
⅛ teaspoon fresh-ground
  black pepper
¼ teaspoon sugar
1 teaspoon dry mustard

1 teaspoon oregano
¼ teaspoon minced fresh
  garlic
¼ teaspoon lemon juice
¾ cup olive oil

Mix all the ingredients together except the olive oil. Let stand for 15 to 20 minutes so flavors will blend. Add olive oil gradually, mixing all the while.

Penne, Sausage, and Broccoli

6 Italian sausages, sweet
  or hot
2 tablespoons olive oil
1 clove garlic, chopped
Chopped fresh parsley

1 pound penne pasta
2 cups marinara sauce
Grated Parmesan cheese
Cooked broccoli

Cover sausage in cold water. Bring to a boil; simmer uncovered for 10 minutes. Drain and dry then slice into rounds. In a skillet, heat olive oil. Add sausage, garlic, and some of the parsley. Stir until brown. Add cooked penne and marinara. Mix the sausage and the sauce with Parmesan cheese and remaining parsley. Serve with cooked broccoli. Serves 4.

Fettuccini Alfredo

1 pound narrow egg
  noodles
8 tablespoons unsalted
  butter

¼ cup heavy cream
1 cup grated Parmesan
  cheese, divided
Ground pepper

Boil noodles in a large pot of salted water until tender. Drain noodles. Place noodles in a skillet. Add butter, cream, and half the Parmesan cheese. Use 2 forks and toss until mixed well. Top with pepper and Parmesan cheese.

Note: You may top with chicken, shrimp, fish, etc.

Veal Scaloppine

1¼ pounds veal, sliced
  thin (leg round or eye)
Flour (enough to dredge
  veal)
Olive oil
2 ounces Marsala wine

3 ounces veal stock
4 ounces prosciutto ham
2 teaspoons Parmesan
  cheese
Risotto

Dredge veal pieces lightly in flour. Sauté rapidly in olive oil. Transfer veal to oven-proof casserole. Deglaze sauté pan with Marsala wine. Add stock; reduce and pour over veal. Place a piece of ham on top of each veal slice. Sprinkle with Parmesan cheese. Place in hot oven. Do not overcook. Serve with risotto.

The Atlanta Metro Region

Culturally diverse, modern yet traditional, friendly and charming, Atlanta is an incredible place to live and play. Museums, theatres, opera, ballet, botanical gardens, parks, festivals . . . so much to see and do!   Of particular interest are Centennial Olympic Park and the Jimmy Carter Library with its replica of the Oval Office and 70 million pages of original documents. Outside of Atlanta, tour antebellum homes in Roswell's historic district, visit the Chattahoochee Nature Center, and canoe the Chattahoochee River. Take a walk on the wild side at Six Flags White Water in Marietta, featuring waterfalls, slides, a 735-foot tunnel raft ride, two lazy rivers, and a 750,000-gallon wave pool. You'll never run out of things to do in the Atlanta Metro Region.

The Atlanta Metro Region Menu

(continued)

The Atlanta Metro Region Menu

Vinny's On Windward

5355 Windward Parkway
Alpharetta, GA 30004
(770) 772-GOGH (4644)

Business, pleasure, parties, patio—great dining is all about knowing where to "Gogh." Vinny's, a slightly more casual counterpart to sister restaurant Van Gogh's in Roswell, serves innovative food with Italian traditions, and is consistently rated Excellent by *Zagat Guide*. Enjoy the best pizza you'll ever have, made in our own brick oven, perfect to sample along with Vinny's eclectic selection of beers on tap. Vinny's offers many fine Italian wines or California reserves, and for the more adventurous, try some imported grappa!

Jason Myers, Executive Chef

Jason began his career in Bal Harbor, Florida, at The Sheraton Hotel after graduating from Johnson and Wales Culinary School in North Miami. He then moved to the Atlanta area and continued his work at Four Seasonings Catering. Jason moved into fine dining at Toulous as their sous chef. In 2002 Jason joined the staff at Vinny's On Windard, which is part of The Sedgwick Restaurant Group, in Alpharetta, Georgia. Working at Vinny's he quickly adjusted to the rustic Italian style of Vinny's and in the summer of 2003 was promoted to his current position as executive chef.

Tuscan Bread and Tomato Soup

6 pounds vine-ripened tomatoes	$\frac{1}{2}$ cup oregano olive oil
$\frac{1}{3}$ cup extra virgin olive oil	$1\frac{1}{3}$ tablespoons soul (salt and pepper)
1 leek, julienne	$\frac{1}{4}$ cup fresh-squeezed lemon juice
$\frac{1}{4}$ cup finely chopped garlic	2 teaspoons coarsely ground black pepper
$2\frac{2}{3}$ tablespoons tomato paste	

Lightly brush tomatoes with olive oil. Place in hot (400°) oven until skins blister and turn black. (Place the tomatoes near the flame so they blacken quickly and do not overcook.) Remove tomatoes from oven and peel off skin while reserving both the pulp and the juice. Seed and roughly chop tomatoes. Reserve juice and pulp separately. Heat remaining olive oil and sauté leeks and garlic until they are limp. Add tomato paste and deglaze with the reserved juice. Add reserved tomatoes and simmer for 5 minutes. Finish with lemon juice. Season with salt and pepper (soul). Let cool to room temperature.

CROUTONS:

1 quart bread cubes	2 teaspoons soul (salt and pepper)
$\frac{1}{4}$ cup oregano olive oil	
$\frac{1}{4}$ cup freshly ground Parmesan cheese	

Mix together bread cubes, oregano olive oil, Parmesan, and soul. Spread on a sheet pan and bake at 400° until light brown and crisp.

Warm soup and pour over Croutons. Toss arugula with soul and lemon juice and place on top of soup. Garnish with shaved Parmesan. Serves 8.

Tuna Tartar with Radish Salad

GINGERED SOY VINAIGRETTE DRESSING:

1 ounce minced ginger	1 cup rice wine vinegar
1/3 cup chopped fresh basil	1/3 cup teriyaki sauce
1/3 cup chopped fresh cilantro	1/3 cup grapeseed oil
1 clove garlic	1/3 cup sesame oil
1 jalapeño pepper	1 teaspoon freshly ground black pepper
Shallots, chopped	

Purée herbs, garlic, jalapeños, and shallots. Add vinegar and teriyaki, then slowly add oils and peppers. Set aside.

2 pounds tuna (freshest available)	1 habanero pepper, finely minced
1 bunch finely minced chives	1 ounce rice vinegar
1/4 cup minced red onion	1/4 cup capers
1/2 red bell pepper, finely minced	4 limes, juiced
1 ounce sesame oil	Kosher salt and white pepper to taste

Working quickly to keep the tuna well chilled, finely mince the raw tuna using a large chef's knife, until tuna is evenly minced into very fine pieces. Combine with chives, onion, sesame oil, peppers, vinegar, capers, lime juice, kosher salt, and white pepper. Serves 8.

RADISH SALAD:

16 radishes, slivered	1 cup Gingered Soy Vinaigrette
1 pint diakon sprouts	

Toss the slivered radishes and diakon sprouts with Gingered Soy Vinaigrette Dressing. Arrange radishes and sprouts evenly in center of 8 plates. Divide seasoned raw tuna on top and garnish with lime.

Lobster and Citrus Salad

This is an easy but truly tasty dish.

1 large red beet	Sugar
4 ounces freshly squeezed lemon juice	1/2 pound micro greens
	2 cups pecans
4 ounces freshly squeezed orange juice	2 cups Mandarin orange segments
8 ounces pineapple juice	8 (5- to 6-ounce) Maine lobster tails, boiled,
8 ounces olive oil	chilled, and cleaned
Salt and white pepper	

Boil beet in a pot of water till soft enough to pierce through with a knife. Place in ice bath to cool, then peel and slice into thin rounds. Set aside. Combine lemon, orange, and pineapple juice in a blender. With the blender on, slowly add olive oil to emulsify. Add salt, pepper, and sugar to taste. Set aside.

Place 3 rounds of beets on each plate. Leave center of plate clear for salad mixture. Toss micro greens, pecans, Mandarin orange segments, and citrus sauce together in a bowl. Place salad mixture in center of plate. Toss chilled lobster tail in bowl with any remaining citrus sauce, then place on top of salad.

Veal Bologonaise

8 ounces finely chopped carrots	Salt and pepper
	4 ounces port wine
8 ounces finely chopped onions	1 cup 3/4-inch tomato concassé
8 ounces finely chopped celery	1 cup heavy cream
4 ounces finely chopped fennel	1 1/2 teaspoons freshly ground black pepper
3 tablespoons minced garlic	Soul (salt and white pepper) to taste
2 tablespoons olive oil	Fresh pasta
1 1/2 pounds ground veal	

Sauté carrots, onions, celery, fennel, and garlic in olive oil until translucent. In another pan, season veal with salt and white pepper, then brown, drain fat, and set aside.

Deglaze vegetables with port and reduce until 1/4 of the liquid remains. Add browned veal and tomato concassé to vegetables and cook on high for 10 minutes. Add cream and reduce by one half. Season with freshly ground pepper and soul to taste. Serve over fresh pasta. Serves 6.

Atlanta Fish Market

265 Pharr Road
Atlanta, GA 30305
(404) 262-3165

Mark Norberg, General Manager
Robert Holley, Executive Chef

Atlanta Fish Market offers a menu printed daily with plenty of healthy seafood dishes. Guests are invited to relax and enjoy the upscale, casual atmosphere.

Asian-Spiced Beer Can Cornish Game Hen

MARINADE:

2 oranges, juiced	2 tablespoons honey
½ cup rice wine vinegar	
1 tablespoon freshly chopped ginger	

Mix all ingredients.

2 Cornish hens	2 stalks rosemary
Salt and pepper to taste	Thyme
2 tablespoons Chinese five-spice powder	½ cup ginger
	½ cup sweet soy sauce
8 cloves garlic, crushed	

Marinate hens for approximately 2 hours.

Remove hens from marinade; season with salt, pepper, and Chinese five-spice, then stuff cavity of the hen with garlic, rosemary, and thyme. Place ginger and half the Marinade into a 12-ounce steel can. Rest hen on top of can and grill at low temperature, basting often. When birds are nearly cooked, finish with final glaze of sweet soy sauce. Cook until dark, golden brown or approximately 45 minutes to 1 hour.

Oysters Bienville

1 cup finely chopped green onions	1 teaspoon salt
1 cup finely chopped yellow onions	1 teaspoon light pepper
	1 pinch cayenne pepper
4 ounces butter	¼ cup finely chopped parsley
8 ounces mushrooms, chopped	¼ cup heavy cream
Juice of 1 lemon	4 egg yolks
¼ cup flour	24 freshly shucked oysters on the half shell
1 cup dry sherry wine	Rock salt
1 cup clam juice	
1 ounce finely chopped raw shrimp	

OYSTER TOPPING:

½ cup butter, melted	½ cup grated Parmesan cheese
½ cup plain bread crumbs	Paprika to taste

Sauté onions in butter until tender in a heavy saucepan. Add mushrooms and lemon juice, cooking over medium heat for 10 minutes. Sprinkle flour over mushrooms and onions, and mix evenly (do not brown). Add wine and clam juice, and cook about 10 more minutes until sauce thickens. Add shrimp; season with salt, pepper, cayenne pepper, and parsley. Cook 5 more minutes, then let cool.

Whip the cream lightly and add egg yolks. Fold this mixture into mushrooms, onions, and shrimp. Place freshly shucked oysters over rock salt and cover with this mixture. Over the top, add butter, bread crumbs, Parmesan cheese, and paprika. Bake in a 500° oven for 10 to 15 minutes, and serve over rock salt. Garnish with lemon and parsley.

Atlanta Fish Market's Famous Bread Pudding

1 loaf Buckhead Bread Company bread, crust removed, cut into 1-inch squares	1 quart heavy cream
	2 cups golden raisins
	2 ounces Italian rum
	1 pound sugar
15 egg yolks	½ pound brown sugar

Combine all ingredients except brown sugar. Coat 10x12-inch baking dish with a small amount of vegetable oil, and dust with fine sugar. Put bread pudding mixture into baking dish, cover evenly with brown sugar, cover with foil, and bake in a water bath for 90 minutes at 350°. When done, remove foil and bake 10 more minutes.

Atlanta Fish Market's Sea Bass Hong Kong Style

4 ounces light soy sauce	2 tablespoons sugar
2 ounces water	2 (8-ounce) portions of favorite fish
3 ounces dry sherry wine	

Combine all ingredients except fish and bring to a boil. (Set some aside for final plate presentation.) Steam or sauté fish with part of this mixture.

1 pound spinach, washed and stemmed	2 tablespoons fine julienne ginger
2 tablespoons sesame oil	2 tablespoons fine julienne scallion
2 tablespoons olive oil	
Salt and pepper to taste	

Sweat spinach in sesame and olive oil and season with salt and pepper. Place a bed of spinach in a soup bowl, rest fish on top of spinach, and garnish with ginger and scallions. Pour reserved soy broth over fish, and serve with sticky rice and chopsticks.

Note: Sea Bass Hong Kong has been one of Atlanta Fish Market's best sellers, and often copied by many other restaurants around the country, but never quite replicated accurately. The recipe is realistically defined, and best enjoyed surrounded by the ambiance, excitement, and sheer pleasure derived from a dining experience at the Atlanta Fish Market.

Mussels in a Marinière Broth

1 pound mussels	4 ounces white wine, divided
1 tablespoon chopped shallots	4 ounces cream
4 ounces compound butter (4 ounces butter, 1 teaspoon garlic, 1 teaspoon parsley), divided	Pinch cayenne pepper
	Squeeze of lemon
	1 teaspoon chopped parsley

Wash mussels; sweat thinly sliced shallots in 1 tablespoon butter and 2 ounces white wine, until tender. Add cream, remaining wine, and mussels, and cook gently until mussels open. Finish with sprinkle of cayenne pepper and lemon juice to taste. Serve garnished with chopped parsley.

Note: This simple dish was shown to me by my favorite chef and my mentor as well, Gilbert LeCoze. It is a straightforward dish consisting of white wine, garlic, shallots, and parsley.

Georgia Pacific Building and Candler Building, Atlanta

Bluepointe

3455 Peachtree Road
Atlanta, GA 30326
(404) 237-9070

Kevin Brown, General Manager
Ian Winslade, Executive Chef

Chef Ian Winslade presents healthy options such as his daily "Six Pack Stomach" lunch special and riceless sushi. Bluepointe's close proximity to offices and hip shopping make it the perfect venue to lunch in style. General Manager Kevin Brown and his staff round out a great experience.

Coconut Chicken Soup

STOCK:

1 chicken carcass	1 bunch of thyme
1 carrot	1 bay leaf
1 celery stick	1 tablespoon of red curry
1 onion	paste
1 leek	

Put all ingredients into a crockpot and cover with water. Cook on LOW overnight, then strain through a fine sieve and remove any grease from Stock.

SOUP:

1 cup shredded chicken breast	3 cups chicken broth
1 teaspoon vegetable oil	1½ cups coconut milk
1 teaspoon finely diced ginger	1 teaspoon vegetable oil
¼ cup diced yellow onions	Juice of 2 limes
¼ cup sliced shiitake mushrooms	1 teaspoon fish sauce
	2 sprigs cilantro

Over medium heat, sweat chicken with vegetable oil until it is almost white in appearance. Then add ginger and onion. Add to this the shiitake mushrooms, then stock and coconut milk, and simmer for 5 minutes. Finish with lime juice, fish sauce, and cilantro leaves.

Roasted Duck Steak on Savoy Cabbage with Panang Curry

4 plump duck breasts	2 cups coconut milk
½ cup soy sauce	1 tablespoon palm sugar
4 teaspoons Panang curry paste	1 tablespoon fish sauce
¼ teaspoon vegetable oil	2 kaffir lime leaves

Score skin of duck breast with sharp knife and marinate in soy sauce overnight.

Sweat curry paste in vegetable oil; whisk in coconut milk a little at a time and re-boil. Add equal parts palm sugar and fish sauce; cook slowly for 10 minutes, then finish with lime leaves.

4 cups savoy cabbage, blanched	Salt and pepper to taste
¾ ounce butter	2 lime leaves, shredded
2 shredded confit of duck leg	

Begin roasting duck breasts in a cool pan on top of stove. When skin begins to brown, remove excess fat from pan and put pan into a 425° oven. Cook breast for 6 to 8 minutes, until medium rare, then place on a cooling wire. Warm cabbage in butter and add shredded duck meat. Season with salt and pepper and arrange on the bottom of the plate. Sauce with the panang curry mixture and garnish with the shredded lime leaf. Serves 4.

Blueberry Spring Rolls

16 ounces cream cheese, softened
1 cup powdered sugar
1 vanilla bean, split, seeds scraped out
Zest of 2 lemons
1 package spring roll wrappers
1 pint fresh blueberries
1 to 2 egg yolks (for egg wash)
32 ounces canola oil

In a mixing bowl fitted with paddle attachment, beat cream cheese until soft and creamy. Add powdered sugar, vanilla, and lemon zest, and continue to mix until all ingredients are incorporated. Place mixture into a pastry bag fitted with a plain medium-size pastry tip.

Cut spring roll wrappers into quarters. On a dry cutting board, lay out a few spring roll wrappers and pipe some of the cream cheese mixture in a straight line on bottom part of the spring roll wrapper. Place fresh blueberries into cream cheese mixture and gently press. With a small pastry brush, place some of the egg yolk mixture onto sides of spring roll wrapper. Fold in bottom corners, then sides, and roll to the top, creating a spring roll. Continue with the rest in this manner. When you are finished, place spring rolls on a tray and cover. Refrigerate until ready to cook.

Preheat canola oil to 375° and carefully place spring rolls into oil. Cook until golden and crispy. Place on a dry towel to drain off any remaining oil. Serve warm

Note: Spring roll wrappers can be purchased at any Asian market.

Buckhead Bread Company & Corner Café

3070 Piedmont Road
Atlanta, GA 30305
(404) 240-1978

**Kelly Smith, General Manager
Cameron Thompson, Executive Chef**

Corner Café has become one of Buckhead's favorite lunch spots, with its fresh selection of daily made soups, artisan breads, salads, sandwiches, and sweets. Stop in for a breakfast, brunch, or lunch you're sure to enjoy!

Fried Green Tomato Benedict

2 slices white toast
2 pieces crispy bacon
2 Fried Green Tomatoes
2 poached eggs
½ cup Grainy Mustard Hollandaise

FRIED GREEN TOMATOES:
2 green tomatoes
Flour
2 eggs, beaten
Bread crumbs for coating

Slice green tomato ¼ inch thick. Dust in flour. Dip in beaten eggs. Coat in bread crumbs and fry until golden brown.

GRAINY MUSTARD HOLLANDAISE:
½ pound butter
2 egg yolks
2 tablespoons lemon juice
1 tablespoon grainy mustard

Clarify butter. Place egg yolks in blender. Add lemon juice. Turn on blender and slowly add warm clarified butter. Turn off blender and mix in grainy mustard.

Lay down bread first, then bacon. Then put down the green tomatoes. Put eggs on top of tomatoes. Pour hollandaise on top of eggs.

Buckhead Diner

3073 Piedmont Road
Atlanta, GA 30305
(404) 262-3336

Jill Pipes, General Manager
Matt Harris, Executive Chef

Buckhead Diner is Atlanta's quintessential fun place to "do lunch." Buckhead Diner offers an updated menu, complete with classics and lighter, healthier dishes and smooth, friendly service. This upscale comfortable favorite hits the spot every time.

Crab Cakes

1 pound jumbo lump crabmeat, drained	1 teaspoon Dijon mustard
2⅜ teaspoons salt	1 tablespoon minced onion
1¼ teaspoons Tabasco sauce	1 tablespoon chopped parsley
1 teaspoon fresh lime juice	⅜ cup panko bread crumbs
4 green onions, sliced thin	1 whole egg

Mix together in large mixing bowl. Portion in 3-ounce scoops. Shape by hand. Sauté in a small amount of oil over medium heat, browning well on both sides, until cooked through, about 8 to 10 minutes total. Makes 1 serving.

Meat Loaf

2 pounds ground veal	2¼ tablespoons chopped fresh parsley
2 eggs	½ cup fine dry bread crumbs
⅜ cup heavy cream	
1½ tablespoons salt	
2¼ teaspoons black pepper	Mushroom Mix (recipe follows)

Combine all ingredients in mixing bowl. Shape mixture in loaf form. Bake at 350° until done, approximately 30 minutes.

MUSHROOM MIX:

¾ ounce unsalted butter	4 ounces sliced white mushrooms
1¼ tablespoons minced shallots	4 ounces sliced shiitake, caps only
1¼ teaspoons minced garlic	

Melt butter over medium-high heat. Add shallots and garlic and cook until fragrant and starting to color. Add mushrooms and cook until soft and most of the liquid is evaporated. Place on sheet pan and cool uncovered until chilled. Use in meatloaf recipe. Yields 2 servings.

Chops and Lobster Bar

70 West Paces Ferry Road
Atlanta, GA 30305
(404) 262-2675

**Emile Blau, General Manager
Sean McLendon, Executive Chef**

Chops Restaurant is known for its upscale environment and prime fare, and is the classic place for a power lunch. In fact, a meal at Chops might be just what you need to close the deal.

Avocado Gazpacho

24 perfectly ripe avocados	Juice of 14 limes or
12 cucumbers	lemons
6 pablano chile peppers,	8 teaspoons salt
hulled and de-seeded	4 cups ice, blend to purée
4 Spanish onions, skinned	½ cup sour cream
24 garlic cloves, peeled	1 lime, quartered
8 pints cold, pure water	Rough salt
5 bunches fresh cilantro	Chilled tequila (optional)

Skin, halve, and stone avocados. Roughly chop cucumber, pepper, chile peppers, onions, and garlic. Put in blender (or vegetable juicer, if available) with water and process thoroughly. Strain, pressing well to extract all the juices. Return strained liquid to blender with avocado flesh, cilantro leaves (leaving a few for decoration), lime juice, and salt. Process to purée, and adjust seasoning, bearing in mind people will have their own salt and lime quarters. Serve chilled, topped with a dollop of sour cream, lime quarters, and rough salt.

Emeril's Atlanta

3500 Lenox Road
Suite 100
Atlanta, GA 30326
(404) 564-5600

Christian Czerwonka, Chef de Cuisine

Red Velvet Cake with Creole Cream Cheese Coulis

2½ cups sifted cake flour	3 teaspoons vanilla
2 teaspoons cocoa powder	extract, divided
1 teaspoon baking soda	1 tablespoon salad oil
1 teaspoon baking powder	1 (8-ounce) package
1 teaspoon salt	cream cheese, softened
1½ cups sugar	1 pound confectioners'
1 cup (2 sticks) unsalted	sugar
butter, softened, divided	1 cup chopped pecans
2 large eggs	4 ounces Creole cream
1 cup buttermilk	cheese
2 ounces red food coloring	1 tablespoon honey
1 teaspoon distilled white	Zest and juice of 1
vinegar	orange

Preheat the oven to 350°, and grease and flour 2 (9-inch) cake pans. Into a medium bowl, sift together flour, cocoa, baking soda, baking powder, and salt. Set aside.

In a large bowl, cream together sugar and half the butter. Add eggs one at a time, beating well after each addition. Alternately add flour mixture and buttermilk to butter mixture, beating well after each addition. Add food coloring, vinegar, one teaspoon vanilla, and salad oil. Divide batter evenly among prepared cake pans and bake for 20 to 30 minutes, or until a cake tester comes out clean when inserted into center of cake. Remove from oven and turn out onto a cooling rack to cool.

(continued)

(Red Velvet Cake continued)

While cake is baking, make frosting. In a large bowl, combine cream cheese and remaining stick of butter, and cream until smooth. Add confectioners' sugar and cream until light and fluffy. Add remaining 2 teaspoons vanilla and mix well. Stir in pecans. When cake is cool, frost it by using cream cheese frosting between the layers as well as on the sides and top of the cake.

Make the Creole cream cheese coulis by combining the Creole cream cheese, honey, orange zest, and orange juice in a small bowl and whisking until smooth. Slice cake and serve on individual plates, with some of the Creole cream cheese coulis, either drizzled over cake slices or spooned onto individual plates. Yields 8 to 12 servings.

Rhodes memorial Hall, Atlanta

Saffron Seafood Stew

SAFFRON BUTTER:

1 shallot, finely chopped	8 ounces butter, softened
1 clove garlic, finely chopped	1 pinch saffron
	3 ounces white wine
1 teaspoon finely chopped chive	

Mix all ingredients together, except butter. Cook until wine evaporates. Mix in butter. Roll in Saran Wrap and chill until needed.

$\frac{1}{2}$ cup mussels	$\frac{1}{2}$ cup cooked, diced potatoes
$\frac{1}{2}$ cup shrimp	
$\frac{1}{2}$ cup scallops	1 teaspoon dried chili powder
$\frac{1}{2}$ cup clams	
1 cup cracked crab claws	4 ounces saffron butter
$\frac{1}{2}$ cup diced salmon or sea bass	1 cup fish stock
	2 ounces olive oil
$\frac{1}{2}$ cup cooked peas	

In a skillet, heat olive oil. Add garlic and all seafood. Shake pan for one minute. Add all remaining ingredients. Cover and boil for 2 minutes. Serve over steamed rice. Serves 2.

Whole Sizzling Catfish with Chile-Black Bean Sauce

This dish makes a spectacular presentation. The deep-frying stiffens the fish, making it possible for it to stand up on the platter, staring at its consumer.

2 (1½- to 2-pound) whole catfish
½ cup peeled and thinly sliced fresh ginger

1 cup rice flour

SAUCE:
1 tablespoon olive oil
1 teaspoon sesame oil
1 teaspoon chopped garlic
1 teaspoon minced ginger
¼ cup Chinese fermented black beans

1 teaspoon garlic chile paste (available in Oriental markets)
¼ cup dry sherry
½ cup soy sauce

GARNISH:
¼ cup chopped green onions
¼ cup peeled, seeded, and diced tomatoes

¼ cup pickled ginger

Make 5 incisions on each side of the whole catfish by slicing on the diagonal to the bone. Stuff slits with fresh ginger slices.

In a large heavy pot or deep-fryer, heat 6 inches of oil to 350°. Dredge fish in rice flour, coating evenly, and shake off any excess flour. One at a time, drop fish in hot oil and fry until golden brown, about 5 to 8 minutes. Using a pair of slotted spoons, lift out fish and drain on paper towels.

In a small saucepan, heat olive and sesame oils over medium-high heat, and sauté garlic, ginger, and black beans for 1 minute. Add chile paste, sherry, and soy and reduce by half. Pour over cooked fish and garnish with green onions, tomatoes, and pickled ginger. Serves 4.

McKendrick's Steak House

4505 Ashford Dunwoody Road
Atlanta, GA 30346
(770) 512-8888
www.mckendricks.com

**Claudia and Doug McKendrick
Owners**

McKendrick's is listed in Tom Horan's America's Top Ten Club as one of America's top ten steakhouses for 2004! McKendrick's Steakhouse is honored to be chosen for the 3rd consecutive year as one of Tom Horan's America's Top Ten Steakhouses. Claudia and Doug McKendrick have over 25 years of fine dining experience in Atlanta and opened their flagship restaurant in November of 1995. The restaurant is located in Park Place Shopping Center which is in the heart of the Perimeter Center business and shopping district in the north central area of Atlanta, which is easily accessible near the intersection of I-285 and Ashford Dunwoody Road. The steakhouse is noted for and serves only the finest center-cut USDA prime beef along with Australian cold water lobster and fresh seafood as available.

McKendrick's Tomato Salad

4 large vine ripe tomatoes, cut into 3 slices per tomato
1 Vidalia onion, cut into 8 slices
8 basil leaves
1 cup Maytag blue cheese crumbles
8 ounces Balsamic Vinaigrette (recipe below)

Build "stack" starting with a slice of tomato, Vidalia onion, then basil leaf. Repeat sequence again, ending with the third slice of tomato on top. Place crumbled Maytag blue cheese on top of tomato. Repeat steps, making a total of four "stacks." Drizzle each stack with approximately 2 ounces of Balsamic Vinaigrette. Serves 4.

BALSAMIC VINAIGRETTE:
$\frac{1}{4}$ cup balsamic vinegar
$\frac{1}{4}$ teaspoon fresh thyme leaves, stems removed
$\frac{1}{2}$ teaspoon sugar
$\frac{3}{4}$ cup olive oil
Salt and pepper to taste

Place all ingredients except oil into blender. With blender running at a slow speed, drizzle in olive oil. Salt and pepper to taste.

McKendrick's Potato Gratin

1 pint heavy cream
3 garlic cloves
5 sprigs of thyme
4 russet potatoes, peeled
$\frac{1}{2}$ cup shredded Gruyère cheese
Salt and pepper to taste

Simmer heavy cream with garlic and thyme until reduced by 25%. Slice potatoes $\frac{1}{8}$ inch thick. Strain garlic and thyme from heavy cream, then pour over potatoes and toss. Spray a 9x12-inch baking pan with nonstick spray (such as Pam). Place $\frac{1}{2}$ of potatoes in pan and sprinkle with $\frac{1}{2}$ of shredded Gruyère cheese, then salt and pepper to taste (repeat). Bake for 45 minutes uncovered at 325°. Serves approximately 8.

McKendrick's Tempura Fried Lobster Tail

TEMPURA BATTER:
1 cup all-purpose flour
1 cup cornstarch
$\frac{1}{4}$ tablespoon baking powder
$\frac{1}{4}$ tablespoon baking soda
$\frac{1}{4}$ teaspoon salt
$\frac{1}{4}$ teaspoon white pepper
$1\frac{3}{4}$ cups water (ice cold)

Mix all dry ingredients, then whisk in water slowly until a smooth batter forms. Reserve batter at room temperature.

SOY-GINGER BEURRE BLANC:
1 cup white wine
1 shallot, chopped
$\frac{1}{4}$ teaspoon cracked whole black pepper
1 cup heavy whipping cream
2 sticks butter, room temperature
$\frac{1}{4}$ cup Soy-Ginger Reduction (recipe follows)

In a heavy-bottom saucepan, place wine, shallot, and pepper. Reduce until almost dry. Then add cream and reduce by $\frac{3}{4}$. Next, turn burner to lowest setting, then begin to whisk in butter slowly (do not let sauce boil); when butter is incorporated, add warm Soy-Ginger Reduction. Strain sauce through fine sieve.

SOY-GINGER REDUCTION:
$\frac{1}{2}$ cup soy sauce
1 tablespoon finely minced pickled ginger

In heavy bottom saucepan, place soy and ginger and reduce by $\frac{3}{4}$.

4 (4- to 5-ounce) cold water lobster tails

Dip lobster tails into Tempura Batter. Deep-fry until golden brown (approximately 3 to 4 minutes). Serve with Soy-Ginger Beurre Blanc. Serves 4.

McKendrick's Sliced Beef Tenderloin Sandwich

2 red bell peppers	4 hamburger buns/rolls
1½ pounds beef tenderloin	½ pound Maytag blue
Salt and pepper to taste	cheese, crumbled

Under broiler of oven or on chargrill, roast peppers until skins turn black (turning to char all sides). Place in an airtight container for 5 minutes (this causes skin to separate from flesh). Clean peppers under cool running water, discarding seeds and stem. Season beef tenderloin with salt and pepper and grill to desired temperature. Let rest 2 minutes before slicing. Split and toast 4 rolls/buns. Divide roasted peppers into 4 equal parts and sprinkle blue cheese on top. Melt cheese under broiler. Slice beef and assemble sandwiches with roasted peppers and blue cheese. Serves 4.

McKendrick's Peach Pie

½ cup all-purpose flour	1 cup heavy cream
¾ cup sugar	Vanilla ice cream
1 (9-inch) unbaked pie shell	
4 cups peaches, peeled and cut into 8 slices each	

Mix flour and sugar together. Place ⅓ sugar/flour mixture in pie shell. Add peach slices. Put remaining ⅔ sugar/flour mixture over peaches. Pour heavy cream over top of pie. Bake for 45 minutes at 350° uncovered. Serve warm with vanilla ice cream. Serves approximately 8.

NAVA

3060 Peachtree Road
Atlanta, GA 30305
(404) 240-1984

John McDaniels, General Manager
Doug Turbush, Executive Chef

Nava is the ideal place for an important business lunch or a relaxed meal with friends. Either scenario will work out perfectly with Chef Doug Turbush's festive southwestern fare and the staff's efficient service.

Herb Grilled Yellowfin Tuna with Jalapeño Chimichurri and Boniato Mash

HERB RUB:

¼ cup minced garlic	¼ cup chopped marjoram (leaves picked)
¼ cup sliced shallots	¼ cup chopped oregano (leaves picked)
½ cup serrano chiles	
¼ cup chopped cilantro (leaves cut from stem)	¼ cup chopped thyme (leaves picked)
¼ cup chopped Italian parsley (leaves cut from stem)	1 tablespoon salt
	8 ounces olive oil

In food processor, process garlic, shallots, and serranos. Then add herbs and continue, slowly pouring in oil until incorporated; finish with salt and reserve. Place tuna in this rub for 10 minutes, prior to grilling.

(continued)

(Herb Grilled Yellowfin Tuna continued)

JALAPEÑO CHIMICHURRI:

¼ cup jalapeño juice	1 cup extra virgin olive oil
¼ cup minced shallots	¼ cup honey
1 tablespoon minced garlic	Salt to taste
3 jalapeños, sliced on mandoline	Cracked black pepper to taste
¼ cup julienne cilantro	¼ cup fresh lime juice
¼ cup julienne Italian parsley	1 mango, diced, brunoise
2 tablespoons chopped oregano	

Begin by juicing jalapeños to produce enough juice for recipe by either using a juice extractor, or grating jalapeños on a cheese grater and squeezing juice through a sieve. Then combine remaining ingredients except lime juice and mango. When ready to serve, add lime juice and mango at the last moment.

BONIATO MASH:

1 pound boniato root	3 tablespoons whole butter
1 cup heavy cream, hot	Salt to taste

Roast boniato root in a 350° oven until it is easily pierced with a knife (30 to 45 minutes, depending on size of root). Remove inner flesh with a spoon and place in food processor; add heavy cream and butter and process smooth, then finish with salt.

6 (6-ounce) pieces yellowfin tuna loin

Grill marinated tuna to rare, slice into ¼-inch slices, and assemble over a small amount of the Boniato Mash. Then, after stirring the Jalapeño Chimichurri vigorously, add to the top of tuna and area surrounding the mash. (At the restaurant, we garnish this dish with homemade boniato root chips and a fresh mango salsa.) Serves 6.

NAVA Blue Cornsticks

2 cups whole milk	⅓ cup sugar
4 ounces vegetable shortening	1¼ cups all-purpose flour
4½ ounces whole unsalted butter	1 tablespoon baking powder
1 teaspoon minced garlic	1¾ cups blue corn meal
1 teaspoon seeded, minced jalapeño pepper	1 tablespoon salt
	3 eggs
	½ cup chopped cilantro

Weigh out and measure ingredients first. Preheat oven to 375°. In pot, combine milk, vegetable shortening, and butter; bring to a boil and take off heat. Let sit for 15 minutes. In sauté pan, sauté garlic and jalapeños one minute; take off heat and allow to cool. Combine sugar, flour, cornmeal, and salt into mixer bowl. Pour half the milk and butter mixture into dry ingredients, and mix on very low speed using whip attachment for mixer. Add eggs, one by one, into running mixer, then add remainder of milk mixture. Be sure to stop to scrape bottom and sides of mixing bowl with a spatula to ensure all ingredients are incorporated. Once all ingredients are thoroughly combined, remove from mixer stand, and fold in the cilantro and peppers by hand using a rubber spatula.

Spray cornstick molds generously with an oil-based pan spray; do not use water-based. Fill molds with mix and bake on a sheet pan for 25 minutes, turning once. Check for golden brown top and doneness throughout. Yields 25 cornsticks.

Key Lime Chicken with Black Bean Rice and Pepita Guacamole

KEY LIME MARINADE:

6 medium garlic cloves	½ cup sugar
1 whole shallot, sliced	¼ cup kosher salt
8 arbol chiles, stemmed and seeded	2 bunches cilantro, with stem, washed
½ cup Key lime juice	1½ cups vegetable oil

Place in food processor the garlic, shallot, arbol chiles, lime juice, sugar, and salt. Process ingredients together for one minute. Roughly chop cilantro and add to puréed mixture. Continue to process these ingredients together, then slowly pour the oil into food processor. These ingredients will form a smooth sauce-like consistency that will emulsify together.

8 skinless, boneless chicken breasts	Salt and pepper to taste

Pour marinade over chicken breasts and coat them thoroughly. Season with salt and pepper, then grill on both sides and finish in a 350° oven until chicken reaches internal temperature of 165°.

BLACK BEAN RICE:

3 cups black beans, rinsed and soaked overnight in 12 cups of water	4 cups long-grain rice
	6 cups black bean water
1 tablespoon vegetable oil	½ cup finely chopped cilantro
1 teaspoon minced garlic	2 cups cooked black beans
1 teaspoon seeded, minced jalapeño chile	Kosher salt to taste
	Pepper to taste

Cook soaked beans in water until soft, approximately one hour. Drain beans and reserve water they are cooked in. Take this liquid and reduce it to 6 cups. When adding rice in next stage, be sure to scrape the thick bean residue that is left on the bottom of the pan and put into rice.

Heat oil in a pan, then add garlic and jalapeño and sauté lightly; add rice and cook while stirring one minute. Cover with reduced black bean water (don't forget to add the bean residue) and allow to come to a boil. At this point, reduce the heat to a very low simmer and cover the pot; cook until rice is tender, approximately 35 minutes. Prior to serving, add chopped cilantro and black beans. Season to taste with salt and pepper.

(continued)

(Key Lime Chicken continued)

PEPITA GUACAMOLE:

2 avocados, ripe, flesh removed from shell, and pitted	¼ cup finely chopped cilantro
¼ cup finely chopped red onion	⅛ cup lime juice
	1 tablespoon kosher salt
¼ cup toasted pumpkin seeds (pepitas)	

Mash avocado flesh, add remaining ingredients, and season to taste.

ARBOL CHILE VINEGAR:

4 medium red peppers, roasted, seeded, peeled, and chopped	8 arbol chiles, stemmed and seeded
	3 garlic cloves
1½ cups champagne vinegar	2 shallots, sliced
	1½ cups sugar
½ cup water	2 tablespoons kosher salt

To roast the peppers, lightly coat them in oil and place under broiler or directly over gas flame to char the skin; this will cause them to blister and make them easy to peel. Once roasted, cover them tightly in a bowl with plastic wrap for 3 minutes. Remove and proceed to seed, peel, and chop them. Then place all ingredients in a pot and reduce to almost syrup consistency; allow to cool slightly, then purée in blender. Pass through a colander or fine sieve and reserve.

Place grilled chicken over Black Bean Rice with accompaniments of Pepita Guacamole and Arbol Chile Vinegar. For a southwestern touch, place the Black Bean Rice in a corn husk that is tied at one end. Serves 8.

Pricci

500 Pharr Road
Atlanta, GA 30305
(404) 237-2941

Maureen Baker, General Manager
Marc Sublette, Executive Chef

Pricci lunch is back and better than ever, serving up your favorite Italian cuisine with plenty of healthy options, including whole-wheat pasta. Try Chef Marc's Sliced Steak "Pizzaiola" with Arugula Salad, Gorgonzola, and Toasted Walnuts—we promise you'll never miss the carbs!

Braised Lamb Shank Stufato

This is a general guideline so don't take it like the word of God or anything. Most of the things can be tweaked one way or the other.

Lamb shanks	Fresh chopped tomatoes
Salt and pepper to taste	Bay leaves (optional)
Onions	3 cups red wine
Carrots	Chicken stock or water
Celery	Fresh herbs
Garlic clove	

The most important thing is a heavy-bottomed roasting pan larger than your piece of meat. Set oven to 450°. Season lamb well with salt and pepper. Place roasting pan on stovetop on medium-high to high heat. Add your vegetables—lots of onions, carrots, celery, and garlic cloves. The ratio should be about half onions and half everything else. Bay leaves are also good to use but not essential. Once you get some good color on these vegetables add some fresh chopped tomatoes (or canned), then add some wine (about three cups), followed by the lamb. Bring to a boil for a minute or two, then add chicken stock (broth) or water to cover all vegetables and meat by a couple of inches. Exactly how much is not really

(continued)

(Braised Lamb Shank Stufato continued)

important because it depends on how much stuff is in the pan, how big the pan is, and besides—you are going to be checking it every 30 minutes or so and can always add more liquid.

Bring the whole thing to a boil and season so it is slightly less salty than you would like because it will cook down and intensify the flavor. Add some hardy fresh herbs like thyme, rosemary, oregano, and parsley. Remember the flavor of the liquid is totally up to you so you can season it with whatever: you can give it a southwestern taste with tomato; you get the picture. Once it has boiled and is well seasoned, cover it with foil or something and put it in the oven. It will take the better part of 3 hours to cook so check it periodically. It is ready when the meat is ready to fall off the bone.

Garlic	Tomato paste
Onions	Red or white wine
Carrots	Chicken stock (optional)
Tomatoes	Salt, pepper, and herbs to
Olive Oil	taste (optional)

Remove shanks from liquid (reserve liquid) and allow to cool. Strain liquid through a colander or sieve and set aside. When shanks are cool, break meat into bite-size pieces and set aside. Chop some garlic, onions, carrots, celery, and tomatoes. Place a new pan on the stove and heat a little olive oil. Add garlic and cook until it starts to become brown. Add rest of vegetables (minus tomatoes) and cook a little bit. Add some tomato paste and cook the flavor into it. Add some red or white wine, meat, tomatoes, and braising liquid. Allow to simmer for an hour or so, adding some chicken stock if necessary. Adjust seasoning with salt, pepper, and fresh herbs of choice, if desired.

Risotto Parmigiana with Mint

3 tablespoons olive oil	2 tablespoons butter
1 cup finely diced onion	1/2 cup grated Parmesan
2 cups carnaroli rice (or	cheese
risotto)	Freshly chopped mint
1/2 cup dry white wine	Salt and freshly ground
6 1/2 cups hot chicken stock	black pepper to taste
or canned chicken broth	

Heat oil in a heavy 4-quart saucepan over medium heat; add onions and cook until translucent but not brown. Add rice and cook 1 to 2 minutes, using a wooden spoon to stir often. Add wine and stir until evaporated. Add stock, one cup at a time, until almost all is absorbed; stir continuously. Rice should simmer, never boil. When all liquid is absorbed, rice should be tender and slightly al dente. Add butter, Parmesan, and fresh mint and beat with a wooden spoon until creamy. Season with salt and pepper. Serve immediately.

Spice Restaurant & Bar

793 Juniper Street
Atlanta, GA 30308
(404) 875-4242
www.spicerestaurant.com

Chef Paul Albrecht
Executive Chef/Managing Partner

Chef Paul Albrecht has worked in Atlanta for more than two decades and is in his third year as executive chef and managing partner at Spice.

A graduate of the Hotel and Restaurant School in Munich, Germany, he began his career in four-star establishments in Europe. He has held the positions of sous chef at the Hotel Beau Rivage and the Restaurant Grand Chene in Lausanne, Switzerland, executive sous chef at the Hotel Sonesta in Washington D.C., and executive chef at the Lodge of the Four Seasons in Missouri.

Chef Albrecht was named 1989 Atlanta Chef of the Year, one of the four Master Chefs of America by *California Gourmet*, Atlanta's selected chef in the *SOS Home Cookbook*, and represented the Southeast at the American Institute of Food and Wine National Conference in Chicago.

In addition, he has been on PBS' *Great Chefs of Great Cities* and *Live with Regis and Kathie Lee*, and CNN as well as a number of other programs.

Chef Albrecht is involved in Confrerie de la Chaine De Rotisseurs, Atlanta's Table, American Culinary Federation, Atlanta Chamber of Commerce, Nation's Restaurant's Association, and the Georgia Hospitality & Travel Association.

Slow Roasted Onion Soup

4 medium-size sweet onions (Texas or Vidalia)	1 tablespoon unsweetened butter
¼ cup olive oil	Salt and pepper to taste
2 bay leaves	Dollop of sour cream and chives for garnish
4 cups chicken stock (or water)	Truffle oil for garnish
1 cup heavy cream	

Slice onions, put on a baking sheet, and sprinkle with olive oil. Bake in oven at 325° for 20 minutes. Place onions in pot over medium heat. Caramelize for 15 minutes. Add bay leaves and chicken stock, and simmer for 30 to 40 minutes. Mix soup in a blender and add cream and butter. Pureé and strain. Add salt and pepper to taste. Garnish with a dollop of sour cream and chives and drizzle with truffle oil. Serves 6.

Steamed Prince Edward Island Mussels with a Lemon Grass-Coconut Broth

1 tablespoon canola oil	1 teaspoon finely chopped lemon grass
1 teaspoon minced garlic	
1 teaspoon chopped shallots	1 teaspoon grated fresh ginger
1 pound mussels	1 cup coconut milk
¼ cup white wine	Fresh tomatoes, chopped
1 tablespoon red curry butter	Green onions, chopped

In a hot pan, add oil, garlic, and shallots and cook until soft. Add mussels and white wine. Cover and let steam for 1 minute. Now add the curry butter, lemon grass, ginger, and coconut milk. Let cook, covered, for 1 minute more. Place in bowl and garnish with fresh tomatoes and green onions.

Chilled Maine Lobster Salad on Jicama-Asian Pear Slaw

1½ pounds Maine lobster, steamed

Remove the lobster meat from the shells and cut in small pieces.

SLAW:

1 cup jicama	½ lemon, juiced
1 cup Asian pear	1 teaspoon chopped chives
2 tablespoons yogurt	Salt and pepper to taste

Cut jicama and Asian pear in fine strips; mix with yogurt and lemon juice and season with salt and pepper.

PASSION FRUIT VINAIGRETTE:

½ cup passion fruit juice	¼ cup diced cucumber (marinated in vinegar and sugar)
¼ cup olive oil	
2 tablespoons rice wine vinegar	

Mix all ingredients together. Place Slaw in center of serving plate and arrange lobster on top; drizzle with Passion Fruit Vinaigrette. Serves 2.

"Wren's Nest," home of Joel Chandler Harris, Atlanta

Chocolate Truffle Cake

(Mascarpone Sabayon, Caramelized Bananas, and Roasted Banana Ice Cream)

EQUIPMENT NEEDED:

8 (4-ounce) aluminum cups

1 hand-held propane torch with fuel canister

CAKE:

4 ounces semisweet chocolate
4 ounces unsalted butter
4 whole eggs

4 ounces sugar
2 ounces cake flour, sifted

Melt chocolate and butter in a double boiler (two pans that fit together; the bottom pan holds simmering water while the top pan holds the cooking mixture). Mix eggs and sugar until creamy. Combine the 2 mixtures and add sifted flour; mix until creamy. Coat aluminum cups with butter. Pour in the chocolate mixture and bake at 400° for 8 minutes.

MASCARPONE SABAYON:

2 ounces mascarpone (sweet cream cheese)
1 cup whipped cream

1 tablespoon sugar
$\frac{1}{2}$ teaspoon vanilla

Gently fold mascarpone, whipped cream, sugar, and vanilla extract together.

CARAMELIZED BANANAS:

1 whole banana   Sugar to coat

Slice entire banana into $\frac{1}{2}$-inch diagonal pieces. Place in slightly fanned out groups of three. Coat lightly with sugar and caramelize, using the propane torch, until golden brown.

ROASTED BANANA ICE CREAM:

2 cups heavy cream
2 cups half-and-half
1 cup sugar, divided
1 vanilla bean, split and seeded

2 eggs
8 egg yolks
4 bananas, very ripe

Roast bananas in preheated 350° oven for 5 to 10 minuts or until soft. In a medium saucepan over medium-high heat, combine cream, half-and-half, $\frac{1}{2}$ cup sugar, and vanilla bean. Bring to a simmer.

(continued)

(Chocolate Truffle Cake continued)

Whisk together eggs, yolks, and remaining $\frac{1}{2}$ cup sugar. Once cream mixture boils, SLOWLY add egg mixture. (If eggs are added too fast, they scramble.) Using a wooden spoon, stir constantly until mixture coats back of spoon. Remove from heat.

Purée bananas and add to thickened mixture. Strain into a container set in an ice bath, and allow to cool completely. Freeze in an ice cream maker.

PRESENTATION:

1) Using a 12-inch pasta bowl, line the bottom with the mascarpone sabayon.
2) Place the chocolate cake upside down in the middle of the sabayon.
3) Lay the caramelized bananas directly on top of the cake.
4) Scoop the ice cream and lay it aside the chocolate cake.

Coffee Cup Soufflé

Oven-proof coffee cups, buttered and dusted with sugar
$4\frac{1}{2}$ tablespoons butter
$4\frac{1}{2}$ tablespoons all-purpose flour
$1\frac{1}{2}$ cups milk

$\frac{3}{4}$ cup sugar
1 tablespoon instant coffee
6 eggs, separated
$\frac{1}{4}$ teaspoon salt
16 ounces whipped cream or mocha ice cream

Butter oven-proof coffee cups; dust with sugar. Preheat oven to 425°. Combine butter and flour and mix well. In a large saucepan, bring milk, sugar, and coffee to a boil; add butter/flour mixture and stir constantly until thickened. Add 6 egg yolks, and allow to cool. With a mixer, beat egg whites to a soft peak with salt and fold into coffee/yolk mixture. Fill coffee cups with soufflé mixture and bake in oven for 6 to 8 minutes. Serve soufflé immediately with whipped cream or ice cream.

Pan-Seared Duck Breast and Sweet Potato Risotto with a Balsamic Reduction

6 (9-ounce) boneless duck breasts

Salt and pepper to taste
2 ounces olive oil

Score skin of duck breasts and season with salt and pepper. Cook breasts in oil in a skillet, skin-side down first, to medium rare. Let rest for 3 minutes. Drizzle Balsamic Reduction over top.

BALSAMIC REDUCTION:
¾ cup balsamic vinegar
¾ cup port wine

6 tablespoons honey

Combine ingredients and cook gently until mixture reaches a syrupy consistency.

SWEET POTATO RISOTTO:
2 tablespoons oil
5 tablespoons butter, divided
1 medium onion, finely chopped
1 cup ¼-inch dice sweet potatoes
1½ cups arborio rice

¼ cup white wine
5 cups chicken stock
½ cup grated Parmesan cheese
2 tablespoons mascarpone cream
Salt and pepper to taste

Heat oil and 2 tablespoons butter in a large saucepan. Add chopped onion, and sauté over medium heat until pale yellow. Add diced sweet potatoes and sauté for 2 to 3 minutes. Add rice and mix well. When rice is coated with butter, add white wine. Cook, stirring constantly, until white wine has evaporated. Stir in 1 or 2 ladles of chicken stock, or enough to cover rice. Stir over medium heat until stock has been absorbed. Continue cooking and stirring rice, adding more stock a little at a time, about every 10 minutes. Rice is done when it is tender but firm to the bite. Stir in remaining 3 tablespoons butter, grated Parmesan cheese, and mascarpone cream. Season to taste with salt and pepper. Serve immediately. Serves 6.

Veni Vidi Vici

41 Fourteenth Street
Atlanta, GA 30309
(404) 875-8424

Mimi Cogan, General Manager
Jamie Adams, Executive Chef

Veni Vidi Vici offers a taste of Buckhead Life in Midtown. Serving Chef Jamie Adam's fresh, classic Italian fare, Veni Vidi Vici is comfortable, welcoming, and within walking distance of many well-known Atlanta landmarks.

Roasted Peach Brioche Bread Pudding with Bourbon Sauce

3 cups cubed brioche bread
1 quart half-and-half
4 eggs, beaten
2½ cups brown sugar
2 tablespoons vanilla

2 teaspoons cinnamon
1 cup golden raisins
2 large Georgia peaches, peeled, sliced, and sprinkled with lemon juice

Spray 12 individual ramekins or a 9x13-inch pan with nonstick spray. Soak bread in half-and-half. Add eggs, brown sugar, vanilla, cinnamon, and raisins. Mix well. Gradually add peaches. Pour into prepared dishes. Bake at 350° until firm and golden brown.

BOURBON SAUCE:
1 cup sugar
½ cup unsalted butter

1 egg, beaten
¾ cup bourbon

Cream sugar and melted butter in kitchen mixer with paddle attachment. Add egg and bourbon. Pour on top of baked bread pudding while still warm. Place in oven for 5 minutes. Let cool and serve with your choice of garnishes.

Garnish with fresh cinnamon, whipped cream, roasted peaches, or homemade vanilla ice cream

Roasted Rack of Lamb with Roasted Small Potatoes

People generally are frightened to cook a whole rack of lamb because they don't know how long or how hot to cook it. This method is very simple in that you do not need any special pan, difficult trussing technique, or complex marinating. It is all done in the pan using fresh herbs and whole garlic to impart the flavor. Using these small racks, they cook quickly and it is easy to determine when they are at the correct temperature. Also an easy and foolproof method for making crispy and creamy roasted potatoes should prove useful, as they make a great accompaniment to many things from fish to braised meats.

Frenched New Zealand rack of lamb	1 to 2 tablespoons butter
Salt and pepper to taste	12 creamer potatoes (small white ones)
½ cup olive oil	4 rosemary sprigs
6 or 7 garlic cloves, divided	Extra virgin olive oil
Fresh thyme sprigs	Chopped parsley

Season rack with salt and pepper and get a large skillet hot. Brown rack in olive oil on meat side first, then turn it over. At this point, add a few cloves garlic, fresh thyme sprigs, and a healthy tablespoon of butter. Lower heat, then start basting rack with the butter, turning over once or twice. Feel the outside of the meat and if it feels firm and springy, it is time to test.

To test, take a thin bladed knife and stick into center of rack and hold it there for 5 seconds. Remove it and bring it quickly to your upper lip. If it is cool, it needs more time; if warm, it is medium rare; if almost hot, medium; and if hot, you are at medium well. Select your preferred temperature and when you are there, remove rack from heat and let it rest for about 3 to 5 minutes, then carve away.

Regarding that nifty potato technique, here it goes. Wash your potatoes well, then cut into quarters. Put them in a pot and cover with cold water, but also, and this is the cool part, throw in a few garlic cloves and some rosemary sprigs. Don't forget to put some salt in the water as well. Cook them until you can stick a knife all of the way through, but not so much that they fall apart. Drain and cool them. This you can do the day before.

(continued)

(Roasted Rack of Lamb continued)

When you are ready for dinner, get a pan hot with some extra virgin olive oil, some more rosemary sprigs, and a garlic clove or two, and put just enough potatoes in the pan to cover the bottom but don't overcrowd. Let the heat do the work and give them a toss from time to time. When they are nicely brown, drain the oil and throw in a little chopped parsley and salt, if needed. All of this should only take about 10 minutes (not the boiling part). You can start the lamb and potatoes and wow, ten to fifteen minutes later you look like Emeril!

PARSLEY CAPER VINAIGRETTE:

1 bunch flat leaf parsley, washed, most stems removed	2 ounces lemon juice
	2 cups extra virgin olive oil
4 tablespoons capers, drained	2 tablespoons whole-grain mustard
2 ounces red wine vinegar	Salt and pepper to taste

Blend parsley, capers, vinegar, and lemon juice until smooth. Add olive oil. Remove from blender and add whole-grain mustard. Taste and adjust for salt and pepper.

Pan-Roasted Treviso with Fonduta

Treviso, which has now become synonymous with this red member of the bitter endive family, is a small city north of Venice that is known for this particular variety of radichio. In the western part of the country, fonduta is a creamy melted fontina, which can be eaten alone with shaved truffles, over spring asparagus, or even over a beef tenderloin. The creamy texture and rich cheese flavor combines with the pan-roasted radichio in such a way that tones the bitter flavor into a pleasant sharpness. Shave truffles on top and one must proclaim that life is good.

1 pound quality fontina cheese, cut into ½-inch cubes	**2 cloves garlic**
	1 rosemary sprig
2 cups milk	**2 tablespoons extra virgin olive oil**
4 egg yolks	**Olive oil**
2 heads Treviso (Radichio Trevigiano)	**Salt and pepper**
	Truffles (optional)

Soak cheese in milk for approximately one hour. Prepare egg yolks and have them ready. Inspect raddichio and trim root end of any dirt or dark color; discard any outer leaves that are bruised or discolored. Cut each head, stem to root, into 4 pieces and rinse thoroughly. In a sauté pan large enough to accommodate all 8 pieces, brown garlic and rosemary in olive oil until golden, then add raddichio quarters. Lower heat and turn quarters several times to cook them all the way through. Season with salt and pepper and leave them in the pan while you prepare the fonduta.

Remove cheese from milk and place into a double boiler. Add about ½ cup milk back into cheese and begin to whisk over the heat. The cheese should begin to melt very quickly and at first may appear watery. When cheese has melted completely, add egg yolks and continue to whisk. When mixture thickens to almost whipped cream-like texture, it is ready. Arrange 2 raddichio halves on each plate and pour fonduta over top. Finish with truffles, if available. Yields 4 appetizer servings.

Aspens Signature Steaks

2942 Shallowford Road
Marietta, GA 30066
(678) 236-1400

When we say "Signature Steaks," we mean it. Every bite of our 100% certified Angus steaks becomes a memory you'll savor. Choose from the choicest cuts: T-bone, prime rib, filet, ribeye, or New York Strip. Each is grilled to suit your desire- perfectly.

Or if you prefer, select one of our fresh seafood, veal, chicken, or pork chop entrées to delight your palette. Compliment your meal with an imaginative appetizer or side dish and round it all off with a dessert you'll want to write home about. No matter what you choose, Aspens guarantees only the freshest ingredients presented with our signature culinary flair.

Mussels

1 quart mussels	**8 ounces white wine**
3 tablespoons shallots, sliced	**1 tablespoon chopped parsley**
3 tablespoons salted butter	**1 tablespoon chopped garlic**
1 teaspoon soul (salt and pepper mixture)	

Mix all ingredients together in a sauté pan and cook for 7 to 10 minutes. Make sure all the mussels have opened up. Remove any dead ones.

Lobster Bisque

4 tablespoons salted
  butter
3/4 cup flour
1 1/4 quarts heavy cream
1/8 pound lobster base

1 recipe Lobster Stock
  (recipe follows)
1 teaspoon cayenne pepper
1 teaspoon white pepper
1/2 cup brandy

Melt butter in a stockpot and add flour, until it is well mixed. Add all other ingredients and bring it to a simmer.

LOBSTER STOCK:

4 pounds lobster shells,
  cleaned, roasted
1/4 pound celery, chopped
3/4 pound carrots, chopped
3/4 pound onions, chopped

1 bay leaf
3/4 cup tomato paste
1 tomato
3/4 cup white wine
3 quarts water

Roast lobster shells at 350° for 30 minutes. Crush all ingredients except water in mixer. Place water and lobster shell mixture into a stockpot, and cook for one hour.

Parrot-Camp-Saucy Home, Newnan

Lamb Marinade

4 cups chopped fresh
  garlic
2 cups chopped fresh
  rosemary

3 cups chopped fresh sage
6 cups olive oil
6 cups vegetable oil

Mix all ingredients together in Robo-coupe or food processor.

Carrot Cake

6 cups all-purpose flour
8 teaspoons baking powder
2 teaspoons baking soda
8 teaspoons ground
  cinnamon
4 teaspoons salt
16 eggs
8 teaspoons vanilla extract
4 cups firmly packed dark
  brown sugar

2 cups granulated sugar
5 cups sunflower oil
2 cups currants
1 1/2 cups finely chopped
  walnuts
4 pounds carrots, peeled
  and grated
Walnut halves, for
  decorating

Preheat oven to 350°. Line and grease pans. Sift flour, baking powder, baking soda, cinnamon, and salt. Beat eggs until blended; add vanilla, both sugars, and oil, and continue beating until blended. Fold dry ingredients into wet in 3 batches. Add currants, walnuts, and carrots. Mix thoroughly. Bake in prepared pans until cake springs back (40 to 45 minutes). Cool 10 minutes, then remove from pans to cool. Makes 2 (3-layer) cakes.

FROSTING:

3 pounds cream cheese,
  softened
1 pound and 1 stick
  butter, softened

1 1/4 cups maple syrup
3 teaspoons vanilla
8 pounds confectioners'
  sugar

Cream cheese and butter together until smooth. Add maple sugar and vanilla. Slowly beat in sugar until desired consistency.

Dick & Harry's

1570 Holcomb Bridge Road
Roswell, GA 30076
(770) 641-8757
www.dickandharrys.com

Goat Cheese Ravioli
with Herb Pesto

6 tablespoons butter
1 clove garlic, minced
1 cup chopped leeks
  (white only)
12 ounces goat cheese
Salt and pepper to taste
A few sprigs thyme,
  oregano, and marjoram,
  minced

1 package round
  wonton skins, thawed
Egg wash
Boiling salted water

In a skillet, melt butter, add garlic and leeks, and sweat till tender. Add to goat cheese; season with salt, pepper, and herbs. Let cool. Place a spoonful of stuffing on each wonton skin. Brush edges with egg wash and fold in half; crimp to seal. Cook in boiling salted water for 3 to 4 minutes; drain well. Serve drizzled with Pesto.

PESTO:
¾ bunch fresh basil,
  washed and stemmed
¼ bunch fresh mint
½ cup pine nuts
1 clove garlic

Salt and pepper to taste
½ cup grated Parmesan
  cheese
1 cup olive oil
Salt and pepper to taste

In a food processor, add herbs, pine nuts, garlic, salt, and cheese and begin processing. After a little processing, begin to drizzle in oil. Continue processing till coarse. Season with pepper.

Sea Scallop Salad
in Passion Fruit Vinaigrette

Olive oil for cooking
6 ounces sea scallops
Salt and pepper to taste
1 head baby lettuce
  (frisée, arugula, etc.)

2 hearts of palm, sliced
8 whole green beans,
  blanched
1 teaspoon pine nuts,
  toasted

In a hot skillet, heat oil and sauté scallops. Season with salt and pepper. Clean and dry lettuce; mix with hearts of palm, beans, and pine nuts.

PASSION FRUIT VINAIGRETTE:
1 tablespoon minced
  shallots
½ cup passion fruit
  juice, or 3 fresh passion
  fruits

$1\frac{1}{2}$ cups extra virgin olive
  oil
Juice of ½ lemon
½ cup honey
3 chives, minced

Blend vinaigrette and toss some with salad. Serve salad in the middle of the plate with scallops around. Drizzle with vinaigrette. Serves 2.

Key Lime Parfait

1 teaspoon gelatin
1 quart heavy cream
¼ cup Key lime juice
4 tablespoons powdered
  sugar
Scrapings from vanilla
  bean

¼ cup graham cracker
  crumbs
1 tablespoon butter,
  melted
¼ cup raspberry purée

Bloom gelatin in cold water. Whip cream to a soft peak. Dissolve gelatin into Key lime juice. Fold into whipped cream, add powdered sugar and vanilla, then whip back into soft peaks. Mix graham cracker crumbs with melted butter and set aside.

In a parfait glass, layer bottom with raspberry purée. Spoon lime/cream mixture over raspberry purée till glass is approximately half full. Sprinkle some of the graham cracker mixture into glass. Fill glass with lime/cream mixture and top with the remainder of graham cracker mixture.

Duck on Maple Sweet Potatoes with Port Wine Sauce

3 large sweet potatoes, peeled	Salt and pepper to taste
2 tablespoons butter	2 duck breasts, boneless, skin on
½ cup heavy cream	Chinese five-spice powder
½ cup pure Vermont maple syrup	Olive oil for cooking

In a pot, boil sweet potatoes until tender. Drain, mash, and season with butter, cream, maple syrup, salt and pepper. Keep warm.

In a skillet, over medium heat, season duck with five-spice, salt and pepper. Sauté in a little oil; as duck cooks, turn up heat. Cook until skin starts to crisp. Turn over and cook 2 minutes more. Remove from pan (medium rare to medium). Let rest for a moment, then slice. Serve on top of sweet potatoes with Port Wine Sauce around.

PORT WINE SAUCE:

3 cups port wine	Salt and pepper to taste
1 pound butter, room temperature	

Reduce port wine over high heat until about ½ cup remains. Slowly stir in butter. Season with salt and pepper.

Lemon Mousse Crêpes with Fresh Blueberry Compote

CRÊPES:

2 large eggs	2 tablespoons sugar
½ cup water	1 cup all-purpose flour
½ cup milk	2 tablespoons melted butter

Combine eggs, water, and milk in a mixing bowl; whisk together. Next, stir in sugar and flour, until batter is smooth. Finish with melted butter. Chill for at least 30 minutes. Heat a nonstick skillet and ladle in approximately 2 tablespoons of butter. Flip like pancakes and remove from pan when golden brown.

LEMON MOUSSE:

8 egg yolks	½ ounce gelatin
½ cup water	1 cup lemon juice
¾ cup sugar	Zest from one lemon
2 tablespoons light corn syrup	1½ cups heavy cream, whipped

Place yolks in bowl of standing mixer and whip on medium-high speed. Add water, sugar, and corn syrup together in small saucepan. Cook sugar mixture until it appears thick and bubbly. Carefully pour hot sugar mixture into mixing bowl and turn speed to high. Sprinkle gelatin over cup of lemon juice and let stand until gelatin expands. Microwave for 30 to 45 seconds to melt gelatin. Mix in lemon zest, then add to egg mixture.

Whip on medium speed until combined. Using a spatula, carefully fold in whipped cream and allow to set in refrigerator.

BLUEBERRY COMPOTE:

¼ cup water	2 pints fresh blueberries, divided
½ cup sugar	

Place water and sugar in saucepan over high heat until sugar dissolves. Add 1 pint of blueberries and gently stir until natural juices release. Remove from heat and fold in remaining pint.

Yucatan Style Shrimp Cocktail

2 cups fish stock
1 jalapeño, split, seeded
2 limes, juiced
½ bunch cilantro, chopped

Salt and pepper to taste
½ pound (26- to 30-count)
Gulf shrimp, peeled
and deveined

Boil stock, jalapeño, lime juice, cilantro, and seasonings. Add shrimp, remove pan from heat, and let shrimp cool in broth.

SAUCE:
1 cup orange soda
¾ cup ketchup
½ cup water

¼ cup sugar
Salt and pepper to taste

Mix all together and adjust seasoning.

1 avocado, diced
1 tablespoon diced onion
1 tomato, diced
2 tablespoons chopped
cilantro
Juice of ½ lime

Juice of ½ lemon
1 tablespoon extra
virgin olive oil
Tabasco sauce
Salt and pepper to taste
Lime wedges

In a bowl, mix shrimp, avocado, onion, tomato, cilantro, lime, lemon, extra virgin olive oil, Tabasco sauce, salt and pepper with enough Sauce to cover. Spoon into a glass and serve with a wedge of lime.

Chili Rubbed Tuna with Green Chile Cilantro Grits, Marinated Tomatoes, and Ancho Vinaigrette

GREEN CHILE CILANTRO GRITS:
½ cup stone-ground grits
1 cup milk
1 cup water
Salt and pepper to taste

1 bunch cilantro
2 poblano peppers,
roasted, peeled, and
seeded

Soak grits in cold water one hour before cooking. Skim any bad particles that float. Drain. Put in saucepan; add milk, water, salt and pepper. Bring to boil, then turn down to low heat, stirring occasionally. Cook very slowly till Grits are tender. Add more liquid, if needed. Blanch cilantro in boiling water for 10 seconds, then plunge into ice water. Squeeze out

(continued)

(Chili Rubbed Tuna continued)

excess water; purée with peppers in blender till smooth. Fold into grits and season.

MARINATED TOMATOES:
2 ripe tomatoes
1 tablespoon chopped
shallot
1 teaspoon minced garlic
1 tablespoon chopped
cilantro

1 tablespoon chopped
flat leaf parsley
1 tablespoon extra virgin
olive oil
Juice of ½ lime

Core tomatoes and place an X on the other side; plunge in boiling water for 30 seconds, then into ice water. Peel tomatoes, split in half, and remove seeds; dice and mix with the rest of the ingredients, and season to taste.

ANCHO VINAIGRETTE:
2 ancho chiles, soaked in
hot water
2 tablespoons shallots
1 clove garlic
½ bunch cilantro

Juice of 2 limes
½ cup extra virgin olive
oil
1 cup red wine vinegar
Salt and pepper to taste

Remove seeds from ancho peppers; reserve the water from the peppers. Place peppers and all ingredients except water in a blender and purée; if the vinaigrette is too thick, add a little ancho water. Season to taste.

CHILI RUB:
1 cup dark chili powder
1 cup ancho chili powder
½ cup chili powder
½ cup paprika

¼ cup ground cumin
¼ cup salt
2½ cups canola oil

Blend all ingredients well.

1 tablespoon oil

2 (8-ounce) tuna steaks

In a very hot skillet, add cooking oil, roll tuna in Chili Rub to coat, and add to hot pan. Sear on each side 1 to 2 minutes. Slice tuna, serve on Grits, top with Marinated Tomatoes, and add Ancho Vinaigrette around.

Bistro Salad

VINAIGRETTE:

¼ cup sherry vinegar
1 tablespoon minced
   shallots
1 clove garlic, minced
Salt to taste
1½ cups extra virgin
   olive oil

A few sprigs thyme,
   chives, basil, and
   tarragon, minced
Pepper to taste

Combine vinegar, shallots, garlic, and a little salt. Slowly drizzle in oil. Add herbs and cracked pepper to taste.

¼ ounce applewood
   smoked bacon, cut large
   dice, cooked, drippings
   reserved
¼ pound mushrooms,
   sliced
2 heads frisée lettuce,
   cleaned, washed, and
   thoroughly dried

6 to 8 thin beans,
   blanched
½ ounce smoked
   salmon, cut into sticks
Salt and pepper to taste

In a skillet, heat a small amount of bacon fat. When warm, add mushrooms and sauté. When cooked, add bacon and warm through. Then add Vinaigrette and warm. Toss over frisée lettuce mixed with thin beans and smoked salmon. Season with salt and pepper.

Van Gogh's Restaurant & Bar

70 West Crossville Road
Roswell, GA 30075
(770) 993-1156
www.knowwheretogogh.com

Eddie Garcia-Guzman, Executive Chef
Brad Patrick, Pastry Chef

Van Gogh's combines a warm, intimate atmosphere with honest, innovative, high-quality American cuisine. Chef/owners Christopher and Michele Sedgwick invite you to relax and enjoy their flagship establishment where style and substance are the name of the game.

Van Gogh's consistently rates among Atlanta's top restaurants, earning accolades such as Best Restaurant North of the Perimeter, Most Romantic Restaurant in Roswell, and Best American Café. On the national scene, Van Gogh's has ranked among Hudspeth's Top Ten for the past seven years and is consistently among Zagot Guide's Top Twenty Restaurants in Georgia!

Crab Cakes with Mango and Goat Cheese

1 pound lump crabmeat	Pinch cayenne pepper
$\frac{1}{4}$ cup flour	$\frac{1}{4}$ cup heavy cream
1 tablespoon kosher salt	1 tablespoon olive oil
1 teaspoon white pepper	

Combine all ingredients in mixing bowl, using your fingers to mix well. Form crab cakes into desired size.

MANGO AND GOAT CHEESE:

3 champagne mangoes, diced	1 tablespoon olive oil
1 tablespoon crumbled goat cheese	1 tablespoon shaved chives

Mix mangoes with goat cheese, olive oil, and chives. Refrigerate for one hour before using. To assemble the dish, heat sauté pan with olive oil to medium heat. Sear crab cakes for 3 minutes on each side. To serve, place mango and goat cheese mixture on top of the crab cake. Serves 4.

Tuna Tartare with Avocado Relish

$\frac{1}{4}$ pound ahi tuna, diced	1 teaspoon minced shallots
1 teaspoon shaved chives	1 tablespoon olive oil
1 teaspoon minced ginger	1 tablespoon soy sauce

Combine all ingredients in mixing bowl and refrigerate for 10 minutes.

AVOCADO RELISH:

1 avocado, diced	1 tablespoon diced red onion
1 teaspoon chopped cilantro	1 pinch white pepper
1 teaspoon kosher salt	1 tablespoon lime juice

Combine ingredients in mixing bowl. Using a ring mold, spoon 1 tablespoon Avocado Relish on bottom and fill with Tuna Tartare. Serves 4.

French Vinegar Chicken

8 trimmed chicken breasts	$1\frac{1}{2}$ cups heavy cream
Salt and pepper to taste	1 cup tomato concassé
$\frac{1}{2}$ cup all-purpose flour	$\frac{1}{4}$ cup shredded fresh basil, divided
3 tablespoons olive oil	
2 tablespoons butter	$\frac{1}{4}$ cup Reggiano Parmesan
2 cups chopped leeks (cut into $\frac{1}{2}$-inch squares)	Linguini or fettuccini, cooked
1 cup mushrooms	
1 cup Tarragon-Infused Champagne Vinegar (recipe follows)	

Season chicken with salt and pepper and lightly coat with flour. In a large sauté pan, add olive oil; when hot, add chicken and cook until golden brown. Drain chicken and add butter, leeks, and mushrooms. Cook until leeks are transparent. Add tarragon vinegar and reduce by three-fourths. Add heavy cream and tomatoes; cook on medium heat until thick. Combine half of the shredded basil and Reggiano Parmesan; add pasta and toss well. Garnish with remaining basil. Serves 4.

TARRAGON-INFUSED CHAMPAGNE VINEGAR:

3 white peppercorns	1 quart champagne vinegar
$\frac{1}{4}$ cup tarragon	

Add white peppercorns and tarragon to champagne vinegar. Let rest for 24 hours.

Buttermilk Panna Cotta with Peach Vanilla Compote and Brown Sugar Ice Box Cookies

BUTTERMILK PANNA COTTA:

1½ cups heavy cream
½ cup sugar
1 vanilla bean, split
2 teaspoons powdered
  gelatin
¼ cup cool water
1 cup buttermilk

Bring cream, sugar, and split vanilla bean to scalding point. Set aside and let steep for 20 minutes. Bring cream back to scalding point. Bloom gelatin in cool water, then dissolve into hot cream mixture. Finally, add buttermilk to cream mixture and strain through a sieve. Divide evenly between 4 (6-ounce) ramekins. Chill overnight.

Unmold onto plate and serve with Peach Vanilla Compote and Brown Sugar Icebox Cookies.

PEACH VANILLA COMPOTE:

2 ripe peaches, cut
  vertically into eighths
½ vanilla bean
¼ cup Sauternes, Muscat,
  or light dessert wine
¼ cup sugar

Combine ingredients in saucepan and warm on low heat until sugar is dissolved. Take care not to boil. Remove from heat and allow to cool to room temperature.

BROWN SUGAR ICEBOX COOKIES:

½ cup butter
1 cup brown sugar
1 egg
1½ cups flour
½ teaspoon baking soda
½ teaspoon cinnamon
½ teaspoon cream of
  tartar
2 cups chopped pecans

Cream butter and sugar. Add egg, then add sifted dry ingredients. Finally add pecans. Form dough into a log, wrap in wax paper, and chill overnight. To bake, slice thinly and bake at 350° for 5 to 6 minutes. Serves 4.

The Historic South Region

The Historic South Region prides itself on its music and literary heritage, abundant agriculture, treasured landmarks, and fun festivals. Named by *American Style* magazine as one of America's top 25 arts destinations, Athens is home to the Georgia Museum of Art and the State Botanical Garden of Georgia. Historic Madison flourished in the cotton-rich 1800s during which time cotton farmers built the grand antebellum homes now open for touring. Augusta is best known for the Augusta National Golf Course where the Masters Tournament is held each year. In Macon, the Georgia Music Hall of Fame pays tribute to Macon's own Otis Redding, The Allman Brothers, and Little Richard. The annual Vidalia Onion Festival in Vidalia, celebrates Georgia's official state vegetable.

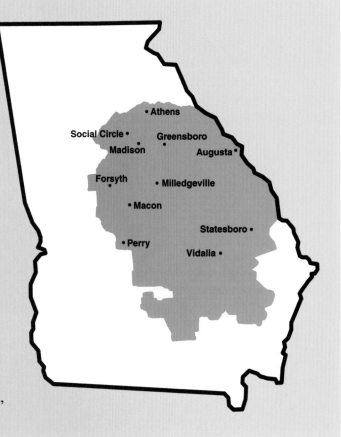

The Historic South Region Menu

(continued)

The Historic South Region Menu

Five & Ten Restaurant

1653 South Lumpkin Street
Athens, GA 30606
(706) 546-7300
www.fiveandten.com

Hugh Acheson, Chef/Owner

"From a heavenly house-made lemonade to a low-country frogmore stew (a shrimp boil) with Louisiana andouille to a really good Caesar salad with apple-smoked bacon, this Five Points' neighborhood favorite knows how to elevate a dish to worth-driving-for status."
—*Bon Appetit*

Seared Dayboat Scallops Wrapped with Prosciutto with Meyer Lemon Brown Butter Sauce and Fennel Purée

BROWN BUTTER SAUCE:

¼ pound unsalted butter	Salt and pepper to taste
1 tablespoon balsamic vinegar	2 tablespoons chopped flat leaf parsley
Zest and juice of 2 Meyer lemons	

Melt butter in small pot over medium heat until the milk solids begin to take on a nutty coloration (do NOT burn). Remove from heat and add balsamic vinegar (careful it may boil over), lemon juice, and zest. Set aside. Warm sauce through when ready to serve. Season and finish with the parsley.

(continued)

(Seared Dayboat Scallops continued)

1½ pounds sea scallops, the largest and freshest you can find	Salt and pepper to taste
	2 tablespoons corn oil
6 slices prosciutto (di Parma or San Danielle)	

The key to searing off scallops or fish is that you want it to be dry. Get the excess liquid off of them with a towel. Cut 18 long strips of prosciutto and wrap 3 scallops (depending on size of scallops) per person. Season lightly with salt and pepper. Preheat oven to 400°. Heat a large fry pan on medium-high heat. When hot, add oil. Carefully add scallops; let them sit and sizzle for one minute on that one side. Then flip and finish for another minute. The scallops can then be placed in the oven for one minute. Serves 6.

FENNEL PURÉE:

2 large bulbs of fennel, quartered and cored	2 tablespoons butter, unsalted
1 potato, peeled and cut to 1-inch dice	1 tablespoon olive oil
2 tablespoons heavy cream	Salt and pepper to taste

Place the fennel and the potato in a pot. Cover with water and bring to a boil over high heat. As soon as a boil has been reached, reduce heat to medium to keep a constant simmer. Cook for about 15 minutes from this point, until both the fennel and potato are fork-tender. Strain. Discard liquid. Using a food processor, purée the potato and fennel. Add cream, butter, and olive oil. Season. Keep warm until you are ready to serve.

To complete the dish, warm the Fennel Purée and place it in the middle of each plate. Top the purée with seared scallops and onto this, drizzle round the Brown Butter Sauce.

Pecan and Pear Flip Cake

4 tablespoons unsalted butter	1 cup sugar
4 large pears, cored and cut into ¾-inch slices	½ teaspoon ground ginger
Juice and zest of 1 orange	1 vanilla bean, stripped
	¾ cup pecan halves

Melt butter in a 10-inch cast-iron skillet. Add sliced pears and orange zest. Cook for a couple of minutes, then add sugar, ginger, vanilla, and orange juice. Cook for about 5 more minutes. Remove pear from pan. Keep pan on heat and finish bringing the sugar to medium dark caramel. Turn off heat on caramel and arrange pears and pecans in the caramel.

BATTER:

⅓ cup unsalted butter, softened	1¼ cups all-purpose flour
1 cup sugar	1½ teaspoons baking powder
4 eggs, separated	1 teaspoon baking soda
½ teaspoon vanilla extract	Pinch salt

Combine Batter ingredients and pour on top of pears and pecans. Place in preheated 350° oven for 35 minutes. Cake should be fully set like a sponge cake. Let cool for about 5 minutes, then carefully invert onto platter. Top servings with ice cream.

Olive Oil Poached Salmon

3 cups olive oil, a good fruity one that is not too expensive	4 bay leaves
	6 thin lemon slices
3 branches fresh thyme	6 (6-ounce) portions salmon, all uniformly thick
12 whole black peppercorns	Salt and pepper to taste

Using a pot (wide enough to accommodate all of the salmon portions in one layer) and a thermometer, bring the oil to 160°. Add everything else except the salmon. (Important: keep temperature constant!) Season the salmon and poach for 9 minutes per inch of thickness measured at the thickest point. Remove from oil, dab off excess, and finish with Lemon Emulsion.

Note: The oil can be reused a number of times, but strain the thyme, etc., and keep it in the fridge.

LEMON EMULSION:

2 cups white wine	½ tablespoon heavy cream
2 branches fresh thyme	
3 shallots, minced	¼ pound unsalted butter, cold and cubed
Zest and juice of 4 lemons	
2 cups clam juice (fumet)	

Combine wine with thyme, shallots, and zest. Reduce by half. Add fumet and reduce by half. Add cream and slowly whisk in butter.

Chapel at University of Georgia, Athens

Last Resort Grill

174/184 W. Clayton Street
Athens, GA 30601
(706) 549-0810
www.lastresortgrill.com

Crab Cakes

6 pounds crabmeat
4 stalks celery, diced
1 yellow onion, diced
¼ cup diced roasted red
    peppers
1 tablespoon Dry English
    Mustard

1 tablespoon Old Bay
    Seasoning
1 tablespoon salt and
    pepper
3 cups bread crumbs
4 cups mayonnaise

Combine ingredients in a large mixing bowl. Adjust consistency of mix with mayonnaise or bread crumbs, if needed. Pack crab mix firmly into a 3-ounce ice cream scoop, scraping off any extra, and roll in extra bread crumbs. Sauté the crab cakes in a hot oil/butter mixture for about 3 minutes on each side, or until golden brown.

Orange Almond Rice

Zest and juice of 4 oranges
4 cups basmati rice
4 cups chicken broth
4½ tablespoons blended
    oil

6 tablespoons brown
    sugar
1 tablespoon salt and
    pepper
½ cup toasted almonds

Juice the 4 oranges that you have zested and add water, if necesaary, to make 2 cups. Mix rice, chicken broth, orange juice/water mixture, oil, brown sugar, salt, pepper, and orange zest together in a metal 3rd pan. Save the orange husks and cover the rice with them. Cover the 3rd pan tightly with aluminum foil. Put rice into a 350° oven, and check it after about an hour. When rice is finished, toss with almonds in a large mixing bowl. Then, put rice in a plastic 3rd pan and cover with a damp cloth napkin.

Basilique Salad

Plump chicken tossed in a Dijon aïoli with basil and julienne vegetables.

10 pounds of split chicken
    breasts
Extra virgin olive oil
Salt and pepper to taste
1 cup chopped fresh basil
2 carrots, julienne
2 zucchini, julienne
2 yellow squash, julienne
2 red peppers, julienne

2 green peppers, julienne
2 red onions, julienne
½ cup grainy Dijon
    mustard
¾ cup brown mustard
2 cups mayonnaise
1½ tablespoons salt and
    pepper

Rub chicken with extra virgin olive oil, salt and pepper and bake at 350° until done. Allow chicken to cool. Pull meat from bone. Julienne the vegetables. Only use the outside of the squash and zucchini. Do not use the seeds. Mix ingredients together. Check salt and pepper for taste.

Bambu on Hickman

2110 Walton Way
Augusta, GA 30904
(706) 312-7777
www.partridgeinn.com

French Master Chef Philippe Chin
Executive Chef

Chef Philippe Chin has won numerous awards, including Maitres Cuisiniers de France 1997, American Academy of Hospitality Sciences Five Star Diamond Award 2000, AAA Four Diamond Award 1994-2000, *Zagat Guide* Best New Restaurant 1993, James Beard Awards, Best Mid-Atlantic Chef Nomination 1997, *Travel & Leisure* Top 10 New Restaurants 1993, *Travel & Leisure* Top 10 New Restaurants 1993, *Gourmet Magazine* America's Best Tables 1997, *Wine Spectator* Award of Excellence 1994-1998, *Esquire Magazine* Rising Star Chef 1993, *Philadelphia Magazine* Best of Philly 1990-2000, and Top 10 Students in Paris 1980 to name a few!

A collaboration of culinary and creative artistry, Bambu showcases the innovation French-Asian cuisine of Chef Chin amidst a backdrop of dramatic décor. The 124-seat, 2,900-square-foot restaurant features artfully presented fusion cuisine, a sushi bar, terrace dining, and an uptown cocktail lounge. Bambu has been booked solid since its debut during the Masters Golf Tournament, and reservations there have already been dubbed by *The Atlanta Journal-Constitution* as "the best in" to have in Augusta next to tickets for the final round of the Masters!

Curried Mussel Wonton Soup

1 tablespoon butter
1 tablespoon chopped onion
1 tablespoon chopped shallot
1 tablespoon chopped parsley
1 cup dry white wine
3 cups clam juice
1 pound Great Easter or New Zealand Green Lip Mussels
1 teaspoon Chinese curry powder
Salt and pepper to taste
1 cup 2% milk
Cornstarch (as needed to thicken)
$\frac{1}{2}$ tablespoon freshly grated ginger
$\frac{1}{2}$ tablespoon chopped cilantro
2 tablespoons chopped leeks
8 wonton skins
Reserved mussel meat
12 fresh whole cilantro leaves for garnish

In a large pan over high heat, sauté butter, onion, shallots, and parsley for about 3 minutes. Add white wine and clam juice and bring to a boil. Add mussels, cover, and simmer for 8 to 10 minutes. Strain. Put mussels aside.

Whisk curry powder into cooking liquid and season to taste with salt and pepper. Add the milk and cook another 5 minutes. Thicken with cornstarch, if needed. Shell mussels and coarsely chop mussel meat. Mix in ginger, cilantro, and leeks. Season to taste with salt and pepper. Evenly distribute mussel mix on each of the wonton skins and fold excess skin into the center. Bring soup back to a boil and add wontons. Simmer for 3 minutes, then serve immediately in soup bowls, garnished with fresh cilantro. Yields 4 servings.

Teriyaki Tuna Loin
with Sushi Rice and Wasabi

¼ cup water or chicken broth
1 tablespoon chopped ginger
1 teaspoon chopped garlic
2 tablespoons chopped scallion
½ cup brown sugar
1 cup soy sauce
2 tablespoons plus 1 teaspoon rice vinegar, divided
1 teaspoon sesame oil
1 (8-ounce) tuna loin, cut into 2- to 3-inch bars
2 cups sushi rice
1 tablespoon toasted black and white sesame seeds
1 tablespoon wasabi powder
2 tablespoons water
1 tablespoon olive oil
4 pieces of nori

In a saucepan over medium heat, simmer chicken broth with ginger, garlic, scallion, and brown sugar for 5 minutes. Add soy sauce, rice vinegar, and sesame oil, then chill and strain. Marinate tuna in chilled sauce for 1 hour, turning it around every 15 minutes.

Mix sushi rice with sesame seeds and vinegar. Mix wasabi powder with water and remaining vinegar. In a large sauté pan over high heat, sear tuna in olive oil for 1 minute on each side. Cut the tuna into ½-inch-thick medallions. Place nori onto serving plates; top with sushi rice molded into a circle with a 3-inch ring or a small can of tuna open at each end. Place 3 medallions of tuna and drizzle with wasabi and Passion Fruit Sauce. Yields 4 servings.

PASSION FRUIT SAUCE:

1 cup passion fruit juice or purée
¼ cup orange juice
¼ cup pineapple juice
¼ cup sweet chili sauce
1 cinnamon stick
1 teaspoon chopped ginger
½ teaspoon cornstarch

In a saucepan, combine all fruit juices, chili sauce, cinnamon, and ginger. Simmer for 10 minutes. Whisk in cornstarch diluted in cold water and bring to a boil. Strain. Yields 8 servings.

Asian-Southern BBQ Pork

1 tablespoon barbecue sauce
1 tablespoon hoisin sauce
1 tablespoon sesame oil
1 tablespoon lime juice
1 pinch ginger powder
1 pinch coriander powder
1 teaspoon chopped cilantro
8 (10-ounce) pork center rib chops
2 teaspoons blended oil

In a mixing bowl, combine barbecue sauce, hoisin, sesame oil, lime juice, ginger, coriander, and cilantro. Whisk well together. In a sauce pan over medium heat, sauté pork chops in blended oil for 2 minutes on each side. Brush chops with the sauce and finish in a preheated 375° oven for 8 minutes. After letting rest for 5 minutes, serve with 2 ounces of green tomato chutney, if desired. Yields 8 servings.

Ginger Crème Brûlée

1 cup milk
1 cup heavy cream
½ teaspoon ginger powder
½ vanilla bean
½ cup sugar
5 egg yolks
2 tablespoons sugar for topping

In a saucepan, bring milk and cream to a boil. Add ginger and scraped vanilla bean. Set aside. In a mixing bowl, whisk sugar into egg yolks. Whisk in slowly the milk mixture. Pour into 8 (4-ounce) ramekins. Cook in a pan with water in a preheated 325° to 350° oven for about 40 to 50 minutes or until set. Chill for at least one hour in the refrigerator. Sprinkle top of custard with sugar, and caramelize with a torch or under a very hot broiler. Yields 8 servings.

Calvert's Restaurant

475 Highland Avenue
Augusta, GA 30909
(706) 738-4514

**Mr. and Mrs. Dan Calvert
Owners**

Fried Green Tomatoes

1 large egg, lightly beaten
½ cup buttermilk
½ cup all-purpose flour
1 teaspoon salt
1 teaspoon pepper
1 cup seasoned stuffing
  crumbs

3 medium green tomatoes,
  cut into ⅓-inch thick
  slices
Vegetable oil
Salt and pepper to taste

Combine eggs and buttermilk; set aside. Combine flour, salt, and pepper in shallow pan and set aside. Put stuffing in another shallow pan. Dredge sliced tomatoes in flour, then egg and buttermilk, then stuffing to coat both sides. Pour oil in large cast-iron skillet; heat to 375°. Drop breaded tomatoes in oil and cook until golden, about 2 minutes per side. Drain on paper towels and season with salt and pepper while hot. Serve with remoulade sauce. Serves 4 to 6.

Sea Bass with Fresh Pimento Sauce

4 (6-ounce) sea bass fillets
  (can substitute grouper,
  halibut, etc.)
½ cup olive oil, divided
2 tablespoons fresh herbs
  (such as basil, thyme,
  tarragon, whatever is
  fresh)

2 tablespoons chopped
  parsley
Zest of lemon
Salt and fresh-ground
  pepper to taste
1 cup dry vermouth
1 cup fish stock
Fresh lemon juice

To help seasonings adhere while it cooks, drizzle fish with ½ cup olive oil. Season fillets with fresh herbs, parsley, lemon zest, salt and fresh pepper. Lightly pat the seasonings on the fillets. In nonstick pan at medium-high temperature, sear fish fillets in a little olive oil (seasoned side down) for 3 to 4 minutes. To form brown crust, flip fillets in same pan and add dry vermouth, fish stock, fresh lemon juice, and remaining olive oil. Cover with lid (or aluminum foil) and bake 10 minutes in 400° oven. Serve atop chive-mashed potatoes with Fresh Pimento Sauce encircling. Serves 4.

FRESH PIMENTO SAUCE:

2 red peppers, chopped
2½ pounds vine-ripe
  tomatoes, chopped
1 tablespoon olive oil
½ pound onions, chopped
1 tablespoon Tabasco sauce

1 stalk celery, chopped
1 carrot, grated
4 cups fish stock (we
  enrich our stock with
  commercially prepared
  lobster base)

In a blender, mix above ingredients well.

Nicholas Ware House, Augusta

Chocolate Almond Mousse Torte

CRUST:
1½ cups chocolate wafer crumbs
1½ cups toasted almonds, crushed
½ cup unsalted butter, melted

Combine crumbs, crushed almonds, and butter. Line bottom and sides of 10-inch springform pan. Refrigerate 30 minutes or chill in freezer.

FILLING:
1 pound semisweet chocolate
2 eggs
4 eggs, separated
¼ cup Kahlúa
4 cups whipping cream, divided
6 tablespoons powdered sugar
Sugar
½ cup toasted almonds for topping

Soften chocolate in top of double boiler over simmering water. Let cool to lukewarm (95°). Add whole eggs and mix well. Add yolks and Kahlúa and mix well until thoroughly blended. Whip 2 cups cream with powdered sugar until soft peaks form. Beat room-temperature egg whites until stiff, but not dry. Stir ¼ cup cream mixture and half beaten egg whites into chocolate mixture to lighten. Fold in remaining 1¾ cups cream mixture and remaining egg whites until completely incorporated. Turn into Crust and chill at least 6 hours or preferably, overnight.

To serve, whip remaining 2 cups cream with sugar to taste, until quite stiff. Using a knife, loosen crust on all sides. Remove springform. Garnish with whipped cream and toasted almonds. Serves 8 to 10.

French Market Grille

425 Highland Avenue
Augusta, GA 30909
(706) 737-4865

**Chuck and Gail Baldwin, Owners
Bunny Duncan, General Manager
Scott Guyer, Executive Chef
Patty Reece, Catering Manager**

The French Market Grille has been voted Best Dessert in the Augusta area for 12 years in a row, Best Restaurant Overall for eight years straight, and Best Place For Business Lunches, and Friendliest Service for two years in a row!

Vinaigrette Dressing

2 large onions (Vidalias are best)
3 teaspoons minced garlic
½ cup mint leaves
2 tablespoons sugar
2 tablespoons salt
3 teaspoons finely chopped parsley
3 teaspoons dill weed
1 quart salad oil
3 teaspoons lemon juice
2½ cups red wine vinegar
¼ cup sherry
Parmesan cheese for garnish

In a food processor, grind onions, garlic, and mint together until finely ground. Combine onion mixture with sugar, salt, parsley, and dill. Add oil, lemon juice, wine vinegar, and sherry to the onion mixture and mix well. Use desired amount on salad greens and garnish with freshly shredded Parmesan cheese. Yields 1½ quarts.

Shrimp Po-Boy

1 quart Wesson oil
2 (18-inch) loaves French bread
1½ pounds white 31- to 35-count shrimp
Milk Dredge (recipe follows)
Cornflour Breading Mix (recipe follows)
Creole Tartar Sauce (recipe follows)
Creole Cole Slaw (recipe follows)
2 tomatoes, sliced

Heat Wesson oil to 375°. Cut bread in 6-inch loaves. Slice lengthwise and remove center of bread. Toast bread lightly. Dip shrimp in Milk Dredge and cover with Cornflour Breading Mix. Fry for about 1 to 2 minutes until golden brown. Towel dry. Coat both sides of bread evenly with Creole Tartar Sauce. Place 8 shrimp side by side on bottom piece of bread; cover with Creole Cole Slaw and 2 tomato slices. Yields 6 po-boys. Serve with lemon garnish and extra napkins.

Note: You can substitute boneless chicken breasts, catfish, soft-shell crabs, or oysters for shrimp.

MILK DREDGE:

1 egg
1 teaspoon Worcestershire sauce
1 cup milk

Whisk together.

CORNFLOUR BREADING MIX:

1 cup cornflour
¼ cup flour
½ teaspoon cayenne pepper
1 tablespoon paprika
1 tablespoon seasoning salt

Combine all ingredients thoroughly.

Note: Corn flour may be hard to find. It should be available through some of the larger grocery stores or fine food stores.

(continued)

(Shrimp Po-Boy continued)

CREOLE COLE SLAW:

¼ cup honey
1 cup Wesson oil
1¼ cups apple cider vinegar
½ tablespoon salt
¼ tablespoon cayenne pepper
½ cup chopped white onion
½ cup chopped green pepper
½ cup pimentos
2 heads cabbage

Combine honey, oil, vinegar, salt, and cayenne pepper in a medium-size saucepan and stir. Heat to a rapid boil. Let cool to room temperature. Add onion, pepper, and pimentos. Cut the 2 cabbages in half and remove cores. Slice as thinly as possible or to your liking. Combine cabbage with honey and oil; mix and let chill overnight. Stir once or twice. (This will keep for a long time.)

CREOLE TARTAR SAUCE:

3 cups mayonnaise
2 teaspoons dried parsley
2 teaspoons lemon juice
2 dashes Worcestershire sauce
2 teaspoons mustard (Creole or Guidens Brown)
¼ cup finely chopped scallions
¼ cup finely chopped white onion
½ cup dill relish, drained
2 teaspoons horseradish
2 teaspoons chopped thyme leaves
1 tablespoon capers

Combine all ingredients in a medium-size mixing bowl. Mix until all ingredients are thoroughly combined. Yields 1 quart.

Seafood Gumbo

BARBECUE SEASONING:

¼ cup cayenne pepper
2 teaspoons salt
2 teaspoons thyme
¼ cup black pepper

2 teaspoons crushed red
  pepper
½ tablespoon oregano

Mix ingredients together well.

1 cup flour
1 cup oil
2½ pounds white onions,
  chopped
1¼ pounds celery,
  chopped
¾ pound green peppers,
  chopped
2 teaspoons minced garlic
1 teaspoon crushed black
  pepper
1 teaspoon whole cloves
1 teaspoon crushed red
  pepper
1 medium piece cheese
  cloth
1 quart water
3 bay leaves
1 cup au jus or bouillon
2 teaspoons parsley flakes

1 tablespoon thyme
2 teaspoons Barbecue
  Seasoning
2 teaspoons filé powder
2 teaspoons Tabasco sauce
2 teaspoons cayenne
  pepper
¼ cup salt
½ pound beef bits,
  browned
¼ cup chopped scallions
1¼ pounds cooked
  chicken
1 quart diced tomatoes
1 quart frozen okra
1 pound boneless fish
1 pound crabmeat (shells
  picked out)
2½ pounds uncooked
  shrimp, peeled

For roux, heat flour in oil on medium-high heat in a heavy-bottomed pan until it turns the color of peanut butter. Stirring constantly, stir in white onions, celery, green peppers, and minced garlic and cook in roux about 5 minutes. Prepare spice ball by adding the black pepper, whole cloves, and red pepper in cheese cloth and tying corners into a ball. In another heavy-bottomed large pot, add to 1 quart of water, the bay leaves, au jus, parsley, thyme, 2 teaspoons Barbecue Seasoning, filé powder, Tabasco sauce, cayenne pepper, salt, beef bits, scallions, cooked chicken, tomatoes, and okra. Add prepared spice ball and roux mixture and cook for about half an hour. Add boneless fish, crabmeat, and uncooked shrimp. Let everything simmer until the shrimp turn pink (about 4 minutes). Serve with rice. Yields 1 gallon.

Peanut Butter Pie

CRUST:

½ stick lightly salted
  butter
1 cup graham cracker
  crumbs

½ cup granulated sugar

Melt butter and mix into graham cracker crumbs and granulated sugar. Shape crumbs to conform to the bottom of a 10-inch pie pan (it should be thick).

10 ounces cream cheese,
  softened
1 cup powdered sugar

1 cup peanut butter
1 cup half-and-half
1 cup whipped topping

Beat cream cheese in a mixer until smooth (30 seconds on high). Add powdered sugar and beat until mixture is fluid-like. Add peanut butter and beat until well blended. Add half-and-half and mix briefly. Fold in whipped topping. Fill Crust with mixture and freeze for at least 3 hours.

GARNISH:

Peanut Butter Sauce
(recipe follows)
2 ounces of skinless salted
peanuts (optional)

Chocolate Sauce
(recipe follows)
Whipped topping

CHOCOLATE SAUCE:

6 ounces chocolate
  fudge topping

3 ounces prepared coffee

Add enough coffee to enable fudge to drizzle over the pie.

PEANUT BUTTER SAUCE:

1 cup dark Karo syrup
½ cup water
4 ounces evaporated milk

1 cup creamy peanut
  butter

Heat syrup and water in a saucepan until it reaches 234°. Take off heat and stir in milk and peanut butter.

P. I. Bar & Grill at The Partridge Inn

An American Café and Steakhouse

2110 Walton Way
Augusta, GA 30904
(800) 476-6888
Local: (706) 737-8888
www.partridgeinn.com

Master Chef Philippe Chin, Owner

The Partridge Inn is Augusta's gathering place, and the place to gather at the hotel is the P. I. Bar & Grill. The logo says "Steaks, Burgers and Music" but that's just the tip of the iceberg. This mainstay restaurant is open for breakfast, lunch, and dinner every day of the year.

Morning starts with a scrumptious breakfast buffet that's topped off by a made-to-order omelet and waffle station. Lunch is served Monday through Saturday and features such favorites as crab cakes, quiche, soups, and salads. The highlight is a grand buffet that changes daily and showcases traditional southern dishes, such as fried chicken, corn bread, collard greens and rice, and beans. Dinnertime offers a broad selection of menu items from sandwiches and burgers to steaks and fish. Meals and light snacks on the scenic verandah are a tradition here. Live jazz is a perennial weekend staple.

The P .I. was recently voted "Augusta's Best" Late Night Spot by *Augusta Magazine* readers. And was chosen Best Hotel in Augusta by *Augusta Magazine* in 2000, 2001, 2002, and 2003!

Philippe Chin's Pumpkin Bisque

1 pound pumpkin, cut into 1-inch cubes	2 medium sweet potatoes, peeled and cut into 1-inch cubes
1 medium onion, diced	
1 medium leek (white part only), sliced	1 cup heavy cream
1 celery stalk, diced	2 tablespoons olive oil
3 cups vegetable or chicken stock	Salt and freshly ground black pepper to taste

In a large pot, sauté the pumpkin, onion, leek, and celery for 10 minutes, stirring occasionally. Add stock and potatoes and bring to a boil, then reduce heat and simmer for about 1 hour or until all the ingredients are soft. Using a blender, purée soup, bring back to a boil, and add heavy cream. Serve in a soup bowl with a drizzle of olive oil. Season to taste. Yields 4 servings.

Drunken Asian Shrimp Salad

1 pound (26- to 30-count) shrimp	2 tablespoons black soy sauce
Peanut oil for stir-frying	$^1\!/_2$ cup sake
1 teaspoon sugar	$^3\!/_4$ cup rice wine
$^1\!/_2$ teaspoon salt	$^1\!/_4$ cup white wine
1 tablespoon minced fresh ginger	12 ounces snow peas, strings removed, "V" notched into one end
3 tablespoons minced scallion (green and white)	

Peel the shrimp. Cut through flesh down to shell and remove vein, if necessary. Heat wok or sauté pan, add peanut oil, and stir-fry shrimp for about 30 seconds. Sprinkle in sugar, salt, ginger, and scallions. Stir-fry 30 seconds more. Splash in soy, sake, and wines. Boil about 2 minutes, or until shrimp are cooked and liquid is concentrated. Remove shrimp and liquid to a bowl, and cool to room temperature. Heat oil and stir-fry snow peas until crisp-tender. Salt lightly and remove to a tray to cool. If oily, blot.

To serve, arrange snow peas around edge of serving platter with notched tips extending a little way into the rim. Arrange shrimp, all facing the same direction, tails outward, in a spiral pattern inside the circle of snow peas. Pour sauce over top. Yields 4 servings.

Note: Hold shrimp, refrigerated in their liquid, up to 2 days. Do not cook snow peas more than a few hours ahead.

The Partridge Inn
Bread Pudding

3 large eggs	2 cups milk
1¼ cups sugar	1 cup chocolate chips
1½ teaspoons vanilla extract	½ cup raisins
1¼ teaspoons ground nutmeg	½ cup chopped pecans, roasted
1¼ teaspoons ground cinnamon	5 cups cubed stale bread (leave crust; plain white loaf bread works the best)
¼ cup unsalted butter, melted	

Beat eggs on high speed until extremely frothy, about 3 minutes. Add sugar, vanilla, nutmeg, cinnamon, and butter and beat till well blended. Stir in milk, chocolate chips, raisins, and pecans. Set aside.

Preheat oven to 300°. In a greased loaf pan, add bread crumbs. Pour in egg mixture and let sit 30 minutes. Push bread cubes down into egg mixture with your hand and fingers. Bake at 300° for 4 minutes. Increase oven to 400° and cook another 15 minutes until well browned.

Cut into serving-size portions and drizzle vanilla sauce on top of pudding.

Building at the site of the Mayham Tower, Augusta

Grits Café

17 West Johnston Street
Courthouse Square
Forsyth, GA 31029
(478) 994-8325

Wayne Wetendorf, Chef/Owner

Chef Wayne is a transplanted Canadian. He began his career as a chef working for a Canadian hotel chain in Dallas. A job opportunity for his wife brought them to Georgia. Wayne worked as executive chef at Idle Hour Country Club before opening Grit's Café. He refers to his unique dishes at his new restaurant as southern cuisine with flair.

Shrimp and Grits

ROASTED RED PEPPER GRITS CAKES:

1 quart chicken stock	2 tablespoons olive oil
1 cup grits	
½ cup roasted red pepper	

Bring chicken stock to a boil. Slowly whisk grits into stock. Reduce heat to a simmer and cook for 20 minutes, stirring frequently until creamy consistency is reached. Stir in roasted red peppers. Pour into greased baking pan to a 1-inch thickness. Cool in refrigerator for approximately one hour or until firm.

Cut into desired shapes. Heat oil over medium-high heat in sauté pan. Sauté until light brown, approximately 3 minutes on each side, just before serving.

SMOKED TOMATO VINAIGRETTE:

1 egg	½ cup smoked Roma tomatoes, puréed
1 cup vegetable oil	
2 ounces rice wine vinegar	2 tablespoons chopped fresh basil
1 tablespoon Dijon mustard	

Mix all of the ingredients well and chill.

(continued)

(Shrimp and Grits continued)

GREEN TOMATO SALSA:

1 medium green tomato	1 tablespoon fresh
½ red pepper	chopped basil
½ poblano pepper	2 tablespoons olive oil
½ medium red onion	

Dice tomato, peppers, and onion in ¼-inch dice. Combine all ingredients and season to taste.

CORNMEAL CRUSTED SHRIMP:

1 cup all-purpose flour	¾ cup milk
1 cup yellow cornmeal	¾ cup water
Oil for deep-frying	28 jumbo shrimp
1 egg	

Combine flour and cornmeal; season to taste. Preheat oil to 350°. Whisk egg, milk, and water together. Dredge shrimp in cornmeal/flour mixture. Dip shrimp in egg wash, then back into cornmeal/flour mixture. Deep-fry shrimp until golden brown, approximately 3 minutes, just before serving.

Place grits in center of plate. Ladle 2 ounces Smoked Tomato Vinaigrette around grits. Spoon Green Tomato Salsa on top of vinaigrette. Arrange shrimp on top of salsa.

The Ritz-Carlton Lodge at Reynolds Plantation

Lake Oconee Trail
Greensboro, GA 30642
(706) 467-7156

Scott Haegele, Executive Chef

Spicy Tomato and Pickled Georgia Cucumber Salad

CUCUMBER SALAD:

3 Georgia cucumbers	2 ounces minced chives
2 ounces celery (brunoise)	2 ounces Cucumber
2 ounces Vidalia onion	Pickling (recipe follows)
(brunoise)	Salt and pepper
2 ounces red onion	
(brunoise)	

Start by peeling cucumbers. Now dice them so they are perfect squares. Do not use seeds, only meat. Now combine all ingredients and allow salad to marinate at room temperature for 30 minutes. Chill and serve. Yields 14 portions.

CUMCUMBER PICKLING:

3 cups cider vinegar	½ cup lime juice
3 cups white wine vinegar	1 tablespoon cracked
1 tablespoon red pepper	black pepper
flakes	1 teaspoon turmeric
2 tablespoons pickling	2 cups sugar
spice	½ teaspoon coriander
1 teaspoon dried thyme	½ teaspoon ginger

Combine ingredients and bring to a boil; reduce heat and simmer for 10 minutes. Strain through a fine chinois and reserve. Yields 64 ounces.

(continued)

The charm of the Old South is captured in Georgia's beautifully preserved antebellum homes, bed and breakfasts, and gardens bursting with dogwood and azalea blossoms.

Peaches were first grown in Georgia during the 1700s. After the Civil War, Georgia peach growers developed superior new varieties which boosted the commercial peach industry and made Georgia the "Peach State."

Centennial Olympic Park is downtown Atlanta's gathering place and lasting legacy to the 1996 Olympic Games! Granite from each of the five continents represented in the Olympic Games is used in the Park. The Fountain of Rings is the world's largest interactive fountain utilizing the Olympic symbol of five interconnecting Rings.

Franklin D. Roosevelt first came to Warm Springs in 1924 hoping to find relief from polio. Enchanted with the area, FDR built this vacation cottage on the side of Pine Mountain while running for president in 1932. It is carefully preserved very much as FDR left it, and is now a museum.

Savannah has become well known for its beautiful parks and historic architecture. "America's first planned city'" was laid out in a series of squares in 1733 by British General James Oglethorpe. Many Greek- and Gothic-style buildings of the era remain intact.

On a clear day you can see seven states from Lookout Mountain in Walker County.

GEORGIA DEPARTMENT OF ECONOMIC DEVELOPMENT

Martin Luther King, Jr. was born in 1929 on Auburn Avenue in Atlanta, in a house owned by his grandfather, A. D. Williams. The nine-room home has been restored and is now one of the cornerstones of the Martin Luther King, Jr. National Historic Site.

PHOTO BY JOHN BAILEY

The first St. Simons Lighthouse was constructed in 1807 by James Gould on Couper's Point. The present lighthouse (pictured) was reconstructed in 1872 on the same site to replace the original which was destroyed by retreating Confederate forces in 1862.

GEORGIA DEPARTMENT OF ECONOMIC DEVELOPMENT

Located off I-75 in middle Georgia, Indian Springs is thought to be the oldest state park in the nation. It was acquired by the state in 1825 and became an official "State Forest Park" in 1927. Many structures within the park were built during the Great Depression by members of FDR's Civilian Conservation Corps.

GEORGIA DEPARTMENT OF ECONOMIC DEVELOPMENT

Stone Mountain, located about ten miles northeast of downtown Atlanta, is the largest exposed mass of granite in the world. The carving of a Confederate memorial on the side of the mountain depicts Robert E. Lee leading his Confederate troops across the mountain's summit.

Thunder Road USA celebrates the rich history of stock car racing. Many experts consider Dawsonville, located an hour north of Atlanta, the birthplace of stock car racing. The motorsports museum immerses fans in the rich history of stock car racing and houses Georgia's Racing Hall of Fame.

Raised on his family's peanut farm outside the small town of Plains, where the family home lacked electricity and indoor plumbing, Jimmy Carter went on to become the 39th president of the United States and a Nobel Prize winner. His boyhood farm is now part of the Jimmy Carter National Historic Site.

GEORGIA DEPARTMENT OF ECONOMIC DEVELOPMENT

In 1796 construction of the Dungeness Mansion began on Cumberland Island. At the end of the Civil War, it fell into disrepair and burned to the ground. In 1880 Thomas Carnegie built the largest mansion ever to be located on the island. The 59-room Scottish castle was used as a retreat through 1959 when it too burned to the ground.

GEORGIA DEPARTMENT OF ECONOMIC DEVELOPMENT

Antique shops abound in Georgia, like this quaint shop in Macon. Many treasures await saavy shoppers.

With over 19 lakes and numerous rivers, fishing and canoeing are popular outdoor sports in Georgia. The Chattahoochee tail water, or better known as the "Hooch," is arguably the best trout water in the Deep South. Wild and stocked trout inhabit both the Chattahoochee and nearby Henson Creek.

Blue Ridge Scenic Railway is a historical train ride that takes you back into the history of the north Georgia mountains. Departing from the depot in downtown Blue Ridge, the 3-hour journey travels to McCaysville on the Georgia-Tennessee border, then back to the depot.

(Spicy Tomato and Pickled Cucumber Salald continued)
PICKLED OKRA:
Prepare the okra at least three days in advance to allow flavors to develop.

2 ounces fresh okra
2 quarts champagne
 vinegar
2 jalapeño peppers
2 cups sugar

8 ounces diced Vidalia
 onion
1 tablespoon cracked
 coriander

Wash okra with a small brush under cool water. Set aside. Now combine all the other ingredients into a saucepan. Bring to a boil and reduce heat to a simmer. Simmer at low heat for 15 minutes, then add okra. Simmer for another 20 minutes at low heat once the okra is added, allowing liquid to cool down.

Heirloom tomatoes and
 3 other types small
 tomatoes (cherry, sweet
 100's, teardrop, or
 currant)

Salt and pepper to taste
Micro basil
Basil oil

Using heirloom tomatoes, take one ¼-inch thick slice and place it in the center of the plate. Use salt and black pepper to season this slice of tomato. Now carefully spoon Cucumber Salad on top of tomato in center of plate. Now you'll need three other types of small tomatoes. You are going to slice one of each and arrange them around the plate in a circle outside the Cucumber Salad. Dress them with the Cucumber Pickling. Now take one of the Pickled Okra and slice it into circles. Arrange the sliced okra in a circle around the plate. Now take on more okra and cut it length-wise into 2 pieces. Use this to garnish the top of the cucumber salad. Now take some micro basil and dress it with a little basil oil and use as garnish.

Bert's
"A great little place to eat"

442 Cherry Street
Macon, GA 31201
(478) 742-9100

Bert's received the *Wine Spectator* 2003 Award of Excellence. Bert's serves lunch daily Monday through Friday 11:30 a.m.to 2:00 p.m. and dinner is served Thursday through Saturday evenings.

Red Onion Garlic Marmalade

8 cups (about 2½ pounds)
 vertically sliced red onion
¼ cup red wine vinegar
1 tablespoon olive oil
1½ cups dry red wine
1 tablespoon dried thyme
 (or herbs de Provence)

2 tablespoons brown
 sugar
½ teaspoon salt
¼ teaspoon black pepper
8 garlic cloves, halved

Combine onion and vinegar in large bowl and toss well. Heat oil in large pan over medium-high heat. Add onion mixture and cook 5 minutes, stirring occasionally. Stir in wine and remaining ingredients, and bring to a boil. Reduce heat and simmer until liquid almost evaporates (about 1½ hours). Increase heat to high and cook 3 minutes, stirring constantly. Yields 2 cups.

African Chicken Peanut Soup

Feeds a large group at the restaurant; reduce accordingly.

2 (8-ounce) boneless
  chicken
  breasts (about 2 cups)
2 cups cooked rice
1½ cups peeled and cubed
  sweet potatoes
½ cup chopped yellow
  onion
½ cup diced red bell
  pepper
2 garlic cloves, minced
1 jalapeño pepper, seeded
  and minced

1 cup homemade salsa
  (you may substitute
  bottled)
1 teaspoon ground cumin
¼ teaspoon ground red
  pepper
4 cups chicken stock (or
  substitute canned
  chicken broth)
1 (15-ounce) can black
  beans, drained
⅓ cup creamy peanut
  butter

Bake or grill chicken until almost done. Chop into small pieces. Cook rice in a separate pan and set aside. Sauté next 5 ingredients for 5 minutes or until sweet potatoes are tender, over medium heat with a little olive oil. Stir in chicken and cook several minutes more. Add rice and next 5 ingredients and bring to a boil. Reduce heat and simmer 10 minutes. Add peanut butter and stir well.

Rosemary Garlic Marinade

1 cup red wine
2 teaspoons fresh rosemary
2 teaspoons olive oil
1 teaspoon ground black
  pepper

½ teaspoon salt
10 garlic cloves, pressed

Combine all ingredients and marinate your choice of meat in refrigerator 2 hours. (At Bert's they marinate center cut beef tenderloin, although any cut of beef or even pork would work well.) Cook meat as desired.

Atlantic Salmon
with Maple Black and Tan Glaze

1 cup maple syrup
2 cups black and tan (Bass
  or Harp and Guinness
  mixed together)
2 jalapeños, seeded,
  roasted, and peeled
2 garlic cloves

⅛ teaspoon chipotle
  powder
½ teaspoon kosher salt
½ teaspoon black pepper
4 ounces olive oil
Salmon

Heat syrup and beer, simmering until reduced by half. Add remaining ingredients, except salmon, and cook for 1 minute, then remove from heat. Purée with hand blender until smooth, and keep it warm. Grill or sauté salmon, basting the glaze several times throughout cooking process.

P. L. Hay House, c. 1850, Macon

Herb Butter

4 tablespoons fresh
   rosemary
4 tablespoons fresh basil
2 tablespoons parsley

1 tablespoon kosher salt
2 teaspoons black pepper
2 pounds unsalted butter

Chop the herbs (can use a coffee grinder to expedite). Whip butter in mixer until light and fluffy. Mix in herbs.

Bistro Salad

This wonderful salad consists of field greens in balsamic vinaigrette with pears, strawberries, sugar roasted pecans, and Gorgonzola.

BALSAMIC VINAIGRETTE:
1 cup olive oil
$\frac{1}{2}$ cup canola oil
1 cup balsamic vinegar
$\frac{1}{2}$ cup sugar (or more to
   taste)

$\frac{1}{4}$ cup red wine vinegar
   (or more to taste)

Combine ingredients.

SUGAR ROASTED PECANS:
$1\frac{1}{2}$ cups chopped pecans
$\frac{1}{4}$ cup firmly packed
   brown sugar

2 tablespoons heavy
   cream

Stir together all ingredients; spread in a lightly buttered 9-inch-round cake pan. Bake at 350° for 20 minutes or until coating appears crystallized. Stir once. Remove from oven, stir, and cool. Store in an airtight container.

Pears
Strawberries

Blue cheese
Mixed field greens

Cut fresh pears (peeled) into small pieces. Quarter strawberries. Add blue cheese. (Bert's uses blue Gorgonzola only because it is mild and creamy. Blue cheese crumbles.) Serve over mixed field greens.

Pan-Seared Halibut with Avocado Lime Sauce

AVOCADO LIME SAUCE:
1 jalapeño pepper, seeded
   and chopped into several
   small pieces
2 tablespoons minced fresh
   garlic
1 cup loosely packed
   cilantro
3 limes

3 avocados
2 tablespoons extra virgin
   olive oil
1 teaspoon salt
$\frac{1}{4}$ teaspoon black pepper
$1\frac{1}{2}$ teaspoons ground
   cumin

Chop jalapeño and garlic in food processor. Add cilantro. Zest limes and add zest to processor bowl, then squeeze in juice from limes. Cut avocados in half and scoop pulp into blender; discard pit. Add remaining ingredients in blender and process just enough to blend, leaving texture a little chunky.

Olive oil
Halibut
Kosher salt
Freshly ground black
   pepper

Chopped grape tomatoes
   for garnish
Fresh cilantro sprigs for
   garnish

Heat a large pan over medium heat. Add olive oil when it is hot and give it 20 to 30 seconds to heat the oil. Season halibut with kosher salt and freshly ground black pepper (or a blackening seasoning mix, if you prefer). Place fish in pan and do not move it for 3 to 4 minutes to allow golden brown crust to develop. Turn fish over and drain oil from pan. Take pan off heat and place it in a 350° oven to finish 6 to 9 minutes. Place fish on Lime Sauce and garnish with a generous portion of chopped grape tomatoes and fresh cilantro sprigs.

Lemon Sour Cream Pound Cake

3¼ cups flour	2 teaspoons lemon extract
½ teaspoon baking soda	3 eggs
¼ teaspoon salt	Zest of 2 lemons
1 cup butter, room	2 tablespoons lemon juice
temperature	1 cup sour cream
2½ cups sugar	

Rub butter all over pound cake pan. Mix flour, baking soda, and salt in a small bowl. Beat butter on medium until light and fluffy. Gradually add sugar and lemon extract. Add eggs, 1 at a time. Add lemon zest and juice. Beat for 30 seconds. Add flour mixture alternately with sour cream, beginning and ending with sour cream. Bake at 350° for 1 hour and 10 minutes. (At Bert's restaurant, they serve a warm slice with an apricot Grand Marnier coulis, whipped cream, and berries). Yields 1 cake.

CRÈME ANGLAISE:

2 vanilla beans	1 quart heavy cream

Cut vanilla beans down the center (the long way) and scrape seeds into heavy cream. Put the whole beans in cream to simmer. Beat cream over medium heat until it just begins to bubble around edge of pot, then remove from heat.

6 eggs	1 cup sugar

Beat eggs, then mix in sugar. Pour just a little bit of hot cream into the egg and sugar mix and stir immediately. Pour a little more and stir again. Pour egg mixture into remaining heavy cream and stir immediately. Put mixture back on stove over low heat and stir constantly for 6 to 7 minutes to thicken. Serve with individual slices of cake.

DANO'S on Forsyth

4524 Forsyth Road
Macon, GA 31210
(478) 405-6575

Dan Pittman, Jr.
Owner/Chef

Dan attributes his love of cooking to his mom, a home economics major. She allowed him to cook and taught him a lot. This love of cooking is evident in his new restaurant on Macon's north side. The restaurant is open from 11:30 am until 2:30 pm, Tuesday through Saturday, and dinner is served from 5:30 pm until, Friday and Saturday. Dan also operates a takeout market Tuesday through Saturday.

Grilled Bananas and Puff Pastry

½ cup sugar	3 bananas, peeled, halved,
3 tablespoons cinnamon	and split
1 stick butter, melted	Cinnamon
1 package puff pastry	Powdered sugar
sheets, thawed	

Combine sugar, cinnamon, and butter. Cut 4 squares approximately 4 inches wide from puff pastry. Slice each square into 2 triangles and place on lined baking sheet. Brush with butter mixture and bake in preheated 350° oven for 10 to 12 minutes or until pastry begins to brown and rise. Brush banana pieces with butter mixture and grill for 1 minute on each side. Stack 2 triangles on each dessert plate, off set, and arrange 3 to 4 pieces of banana on top; drizzle with butter mixture. Garnish with cinnamon and powdered sugar.

Hot Bacon Raspberry Wheat Beer Dressing

½ cup chopped bacon
¼ cup chopped sweet
  onion (Vidalia)
1 cup balsamic vinegar

¼ cup brown sugar
1 cup raspberry wheat
  beer

Cook bacon and onion together in large pan until bacon is crispy. Add vinegar and sugar and allow to come to a low boil, stirring regularly. Simmer until mixture begins to reduce. Add beer, reduce heat, and allow to cook for another 10 to 15 minutes. Ladle warm dressing over baby spinach salad and top with blue cheese or Gorgonzola crumbles.

Feta and Peppercorn Crusted Pork

1 (1-pound) pork
  tenderloin
Olive oil
1 cup crumbled feta cheese

3 tablespoons black
  peppercorns

Rub pork loin with just enough oil to lightly coat. Combine feta and peppercorns together in small bowl. Place pork loin in a foil-lined, shallow roasting pan and firmly press cheese mixture evenly onto pork until coated. Bake at 350° until inside temperature reaches 145° to 150°. Remove from oven and allow to rest for 10 to 15 minutes. Slice and arrange on platter.

Mussels in Chardonnay

4 tablespoons butter
4 shallots, minced
2 garlic cloves, minced
Red pepper flakes

2 cups Chardonnay
2 sprigs thyme
2 bay leaves
4 pounds mussels

Sauté butter, shallots, garlic, and pepper flakes. Add Chardonnay, thyme, and bay leaves. Bring to a boil, then add mussels. Cover and cook on high for 5 minutes. Shake 1 to 2 times during cooking. Remove from heat. Discard herbs and serve immediately with crusty bread.

The Atrium Restaurant

220 West Washington Street
Madison, GA 30650
(706) 752-1445

Aziz Nadif
Executive Chef/Owner

A native of Morocco, Aziz graduated from the French Culinary School in Casablanca, and went on to gain experience in kitchens all over the world, moving from North Africa to Asia to Europe to the United States. In 1997, he joined the Marriott team at Chateau Elan as a spa chef (because of this experience, he is big on healthy foods) and eventually moved to Athens to work as the executive chef of the Hoyt House for almost two years before opening the Atrium Restaurant. Aziz considers creating food, both at home and in his restaurants, to be a work of art, blending ingredients to come up with a unique creation. And he considers creating these works of art to be a stress-reliever. "We spend a lot of time under stress, getting things straight," he says. "At work, you cook for people to enjoy and at home you cook for your family and yourself to enjoy."

Apple Soup

16 apples, cored and chopped	¼ cup maple syrup
2 cups water	1 tablespoon arrowroot
½ tablespoon grated lemon peel	1 tablespoon lemon juice
	¼ cup white wine
1 (1-inch) cinnamon stick, wrapped in cheese cloth	½ cup sour cream

Simmer apples, water, lemon peel, cinnamon, and maple syrup until apples are tender, about 20 minutes. Remove cinnamon. Purée soup in blender; return to saucepan. Remove about a cup of liquid and combine it with arrowroot. When thickened, return to soup. Stir in lemon juice and wine. Heat through. Serve with a spoonful of sour cream on each bowl. Serves 6.

Seared Ahi Tuna

1½ pounds tuna	½ pound celery
¾ cup dry mustard	½ pound diakon root
2 ounces Dijon mustard	8 ounces Cajun spice
4 ounces beer	6 ounces pickled ginger
¾ cup soy sauce	1 bunch cilantro
1 pound carrots	

Trim tuna and cut off any skin. Then cut into 4-ounce portions. Prepare sauce by combining dry mustard, Dijon mustard, beer, and soy sauce into a mixing bowl and blending well. Peel carrots and cut into 2-inch long pieces. Then cut into thin slices. Trim leaves from celery and cut into 2-inch long pieces. Then cut into strips. Peel diakon root and cut into 2-inch long pieces. Then cut into thin strips. Combine 3 vegetables together. Blend well. Roll cut tuna pieces in the Cajun spice and sear rare in a skillet. Remove tuna from pan and slice into thin slices. Place 1½ ounces of sauce on a plate, and place cut tuna on top. Garnish with pickled ginger and cilantro. Serves 4.

Mushroom Strudel

3 tablespoons butter	½ cup shredded mozzarella cheese
1 large onion, chopped	
⅓ cup diced sweet red pepper	¼ cup minced fresh parsley
2 cloves garlic, minced	2 tablespoons fine bread crumbs
7 cups sliced mushrooms	
½ teaspoon salt	8 sheets phyllo pastry
½ teaspoon pepper	⅓ cup clarified butter
½ teaspoon thyme	2 teaspoons Dijon mustard
2 teaspoons lemon juice	
½ cup diced Black Forest ham	¼ cup grated Parmesan cheese

In large frying pan, melt 3 tablespoons butter over medium heat. Cook onion, red pepper, and garlic until softened, about 5 minutes. Add mushrooms, increase heat to medium high, and cook, stirring often, until mushrooms are tender and all moisture has evaporated. Season with salt, pepper, thyme, and lemon juice. Remove from heat; stir in ham, mozzarella cheese, parsley, and bread crumbs. Taste and adjust seasoning. Let cool.

Divide mushroom filling in 2 portions. Brush 4 sheets of phyllo pastry lightly with clarified butter; stack neatly one on top of the other. About 1 inch from one long edge of phyllo pastry, spread half of mustard in a 2-inch wide strip, leaving a 1-inch border on both sides. Over mustard, spread half of the mushroom filling. Dust filling and phyllo pastry with half the Parmesan cheese. Turn up bottom edge of pastry over mushroom filling; turn both side edges. Brush this exposed phyllo pastry on bottom with edges with clarified butter. Roll up, jellyroll fashion, loosely but compactly. Place, seam down, on baking sheet. Repeat with remaining phyllo pastry, butter, filling, and Parmesan cheese. Brush top with butter; with sharp knife, cut 8 slits on diagonal on top of each roll, through top 2 layers of phyllo pastry. Bake at 375° for about 25 minutes or until pastry is golden and crisp. Let cool for about 5 minutes before slicing. Serves 16.

Antebellum Inn

200 N Columbia Street
Milledgeville, GA 31061
(478) 454-5400
www.antebelluminn.com

Dianne Johnson, Owner

This beautiful circa 1890 Greek Revival home is located on the Antebellum Trail in Historic Downtown Milledgeville . . . an area which boasts a wealth of well-preserved Greek Rival, Classic Revival, and Victorian homes and buildings.

Our guests receive the very best of everything. The Antebellum Inn has two parlors, an elegant dining room, a wrap-around porch with rocking chairs, a full-size swimming pool and five spacious and unique bedrooms (several with antique clawfoot bathtubs.) Every bed is covered with luxurious linens and down comforters and guests are pampered with every convenience.

Traditional Eggs Benedict

2 Holland rusks per person (or 2 halves toasted English muffins)
2 slices Canadian bacon per person
2 poached eggs per person
Hollandaise Sauce

On each rusk or muffin, place a slice of bacon, then a poached egg. Top with Hollandaise Sauce.

HOLLANDAISE SAUCE:
4 large egg yolks
2 tablespoons lemon juice
¼ teaspoon salt
Dash of white pepper
2 sticks unsalted butter

Place egg yolks, lemon juice, salt, and white pepper in food processor. Melt butter gently over medium-low heat until completely melted. Remove from heat. Just before you need the finished sauce, turn heat to high and bring butter to a rolling boil. Do not allow butter to brown.

With food processor running, pour boiling butter in a steady stream. Run blender for about 10 more seconds. If sauce is too thick, you can add 1 tablespoon water. Enjoy!

VARIATIONS:
Florenetine - add a layer of Stouffer's Spinach Soufflé on top of the Canadian bacon, then top with the poached egg and Hollandaise Sauce.

Mushroom - sauté 3 to 4 ounces of sliced mushrooms and add to Traditional Eggs Benedict.

Artichoke - to Traditional Eggs Benedict, add 2 sliced artichoke bottoms on each muffin.

Country - instead of Canadian bacon, use a large pattie of fried sausage.

Bananas Foster French Toast

3 large eggs
½ cup half-and-half
4 tablespoons banana
  liqueur, or 1 teaspoon
  banana extract, divided
2 slices Italian bread,
  sliced 1 inch thick
5 tablespoons light
  brown sugar

2 tablespoons unsalted
  butter
Dash of cinnamon
2 tablespoons dark rum
Butter
1 large ripe banana,
  peeled, cut in half, and
  sliced lengthwise

Whisk together eggs, half-and-half, and 2 tablespoons banana liqueur. Soak bread slices for 15 to 20 minutes. (You can also give them a gentle squeeze to give the soaking a kick-start.)

While the bread is soaking, melt brown sugar and butter in a flat skillet. Sprinkle with cinnamon. Pour in remaining 2 tablespoons banana liqueur and rum. Simmer gently and stir for about 1 minute.

In a buttered skillet over low to medium-low heat, cook soaked bread slices 8 to 10 minutes, then turn and cook for about 5 more minutes. You want it golden brown and it should start to puff up when cooked through. Just before toast is done, melt a little butter in a small skillet and add the banana slices. Sauté over low heat for a minute on both sides, just until banana is tender and starting to brown. Pour sauce over banana pieces. Plate your toast and arrange 2 banana pieces on each. Top with the sauce. Serves 2.

Philly Steak & Cheese Frittata

1 medium onion, cut into
  small wedges
1 bell pepper, cut into
  strips
2 tablespoons butter
12 ounces deli roast beef,
  cut into ½-inch strips
½ cup each shredded
  Pepper Jack and Swiss
  cheese

½ teaspoon salt
¼ teaspoon black pepper
½ cup whipping cream
10 eggs, beaten
Ranch dressing (optional)

Preheat oven to 375°. Sauté onion and bell pepper in butter in a 10-inch sauté pan over medium heat until wilted. Add roast beef and sauté about 1 minute. Remove from heat. Top with shredded cheeses. Whisk salt, pepper, and whipping cream into eggs. Pour over roast beef mixture. Return to heat and stir slightly until eggs begin to set. Place in preheated oven and bake for 20 to 25 minutes, or until completely set. Cut into 4 to 6 wedges and place on plates. Drizzle a little ranch dressing over each slice.

Apple French Toast

7 large eggs
1¼ cups milk or
  half-and-half
6 (1-inch) slices
  Italian or French bread
1 teaspoon vanilla
1 stick unsalted butter
2 tablespoons light Karo
  syrup
1 cup light brown sugar
2 Granny Smith apples,
  peeled, cored, and sliced
6 disposable or regular
  mini loaf pans

Beat eggs with milk and vanilla. Place bread slices in a pan large enough to hold them. Pour egg mixture over bread and let soak 15 to 20 minutes, turning once or twice. Melt butter with syrup and brown sugar, stirring until smooth. Divide between the six pans. Spray pans with nonstick spray. Don't skip this step!

Lay apple slices, overlapping, on caramel mixture in the pans. Top with soaked bread slices. Bake at 350° for 40 to 45 minutes. While baking, the apple juices combine with the caramel layer to make the syrup. Carefully up-end each pan onto a plate. The apple slices are neatly arranged on top of the toast.

Tip on slicing apples: take a melon baller and scoop out the stem end and the blossom end of the apple. Peel the apple. Cut the apple in half vertically. Use the melon baller to take out the seed cavity. Lay the apples on the flat side and cut vertical slices approximately ⅛ inch thick. Makes 3 servings per small apple and 4 for a larger one.

119 Chops

119 S. Wayne Street
Milledgeville, GA 31062
(478) 452-8119

Gary Graham, Executive Chef
Will Jarriel, General Manager

Mocha Bourbon Pecan Pie

This recipe is by Jim Souter, in-house baker.

2 cups toasted and
  chopped pecans
¼ cup Belgian chocolate
  morsels
1 (10-inch) deep-dish,
  unbaked pie shell

Preheat oven to 400°. Pat pecans and chocolate in bottom of pie shell, dispersing evenly.

¼ cup bread flour
¼ cup sugar
1 cup dark Karo syrup
4 eggs, beaten
Pinch of salt
1 tablespoon vanilla
1 ounce bourbon
1 teaspoon espresso
  powder

Mix flour and sugar in a bowl, then add Karo syrup and mix completely. Add beaten eggs, salt, vanilla, bourbon, and espresso powder and mix thoroughly. Pour into pie shell; bake in preheated oven for 50 minutes or until pie rises in center. Serve warm, topped with vanilla bean ice cream and drizzled with chocolate syrup.

Horseradish-Stuffed, Bacon-Wrapped, Barbecued Shrimp

½ cup prepared horseradish	All-purpose flour as needed
2 tablespoons mayonnaise	1 pound (26- to 30-count) shrimp, peeled, deveined, and butterflied
1 cup panko bread crumbs	
1 tablespoon chopped chives	
1 tablespoon salt and pepper	14 pieces bacon, sliced in half
	1 cup Barbecue Sauce

Combine horseradish, mayonnaise, bread crumbs, chives, salt and pepper. Mix well with a spoon for 1 minute, until bread crumbs start to absorb water; thicken with a little flour as needed. Stuff butterflied shrimp with about a tablespoon of horseradish mixture. Then roll each shrimp in half a slice of bacon. Line shrimp on board, one over another, with tails in opposite directions. Skewer stacks of 5 shrimp and grill for 2 to 4 minutes per side. Dress each shrimp with a little Barbecue Sauce. Enjoy!

BARBECUE SAUCE:

¼ cup olive oil	¼ cup honey
3 shallots, chopped	¼ cup brown sugar
5 cloves garlic, chopped	¼ cup Lea & Perrons Worcestershire Sauce
3 teaspoons chili powder	
1½ teaspoons cayenne pepper	2 tablespoons soy sauce
	4 cups red wine vinegar
2 teaspoons Chef Paul Prudhomme's Blackened Redfish Magic	2 cups ketchup
	½ pound butter
	¼ cup chopped parsley
4 medium tomatoes, coarsely chopped	

Put oil in a hot pot. Add onion and garlic; sauté till translucent. Add next 4 ingredients and cook for one minute. Add tomatoes and cook 10 minutes, stirring occasionally. Add next 5 ingredients and reduce by half. Add ketchup and cook 10 more minutes, stirring occasionally. Blend in blender in 2 batches, adding ¼ pound butter in each batch. Stir in parsley at the end. Recipe may be halved. Store unused portion in refrigerator for later use.

Jim Beam Glazed Pork Chops

4 French-cut pork chops

MARINADE:

1 cup Jim Beam bourbon	½ cup brown sugar
2 cups soy sauce	½ cup black peppercorns

Combine marinade ingredients in a bowl and add pork chops. Cover, place in refrigerator, and allow to marinate overnight. Grill to internal temperature of 160°. Top with Glaze and serve.

GLAZE:

¼ cup Jim Beam bourbon	2 teaspoons sage
¼ honey	1 clove garlic, minced
¼ cup soy sauce	

Boil bourbon and ignite to burn off alcohol. Add honey and soy sauce. Cook 5 minutes or until it coats a spoon. Stir in sage and garlic.

Priester's Pecans

I-75 Exit 134
Perry, GA 31069
(800) 277-3226
www.priester.com

Crunch-Topped Sweet Potato Casserole

3 full cups cooked, whipped sweet potatoes	1 cup granulated sugar
$\frac{1}{2}$ cup margarine, melted	$\frac{1}{2}$ Granny Smith apple, finely diced
1 teaspoon vanilla	$\frac{1}{2}$ cup raisins
2 eggs, well beaten	2 tablespoons bourbon (optional)
$\frac{1}{3}$ cup milk or Pet evaporated milk	

In a large bowl, mix all casserole ingredients until very well blended.

TOPPING:

1 cup light brown sugar	1 cup chopped pecans
$\frac{1}{2}$ cup plain flour	$\frac{1}{3}$ cup margarine, melted

In a medium bowl, mix all ingredients. Prepare a 9x13-inch baking dish with nonstick spray. Spread sweet potato mixture in dish, then sprinkle with Topping. Bake, uncovered, at 350° for 25 minutes.

Note: Potatoes taste best if baked rather than boiled.

Ellen's Sour Cream Corn Bread

A favorite of Ellen Ellis Burkett, one of the family owners and managers of Priester's Pecan Company, plus a wife and mother. The recipe is outstanding for taste and on-the-go ease!

1 cup self-rising cornmeal mix	1 cup sour cream
	3 eggs, well beaten
1 (8$\frac{3}{4}$-ounce) can cream-style corn	$\frac{1}{2}$ cup vegetable oil

Preheat oven to 350°. In a medium bowl, mix all ingredients until well blended. Prepare an 8x8-inch baking pan with nonstick spray. Pour mixture into pan, and bake in preheated oven for 35 to 40 minutes or until lightly browned. Cut in squares to serve hot.

Hot Fruit Casserole

1 (20-ounce) can pineapple chunks	1 (10-ounce) jar maraschino cherries
1 (29-ounce) can peach halves	$\frac{1}{4}$ to $\frac{1}{3}$ cup brown sugar Cinnamon to sprinkle
1 (29-ounce) can pear halves	$\frac{1}{4}$ cup dry sweet wine (optional)
2 (16-ounce) cans Mandarin oranges	$\frac{1}{3}$ cup cornstarch

First, select only two of your favorite fruits; drain their juices in a bowl, and reserve. Drain all of the remaining fruits, and discard their liquid. Prepare a shallow 9x13-inch baking dish with nonstick spray. Arrange fruit in bottom of baking dish and sprinkle with brown sugar and small amount of cinnamon. Bake, uncovered, at 350° for 30 to 40 minutes. Remove baking dish from oven. In a small bowl, stir $\frac{3}{4}$ cup of reserved fruit juice and wine into cornstarch until mixture is smooth. (May use 1 cup of reserved fruit juice without the wine.) Pour cornstarch mixture over fruit, and return baking dish to oven to bake an additional 10 minutes or until fruit is glazed.

Note: The canned fruit can be in natural juices or in heavy syrup.

The Blue Willow Inn

294 North Cherokee Road
Social Circle, GA 30025
(770) 464-2131

**Louis and Billie Van Dyke
Owners**

The Blue Willow Inn has been voted best small-town restaurant in the South by *Southern Living* magazine five years in a row. Tara, the southern mansion in *Gone With the Wind*, may have been inspired by the Blue Willow Inn. Margaret Mitchell frequently visited Social Circle and was briefly married to the cousin of the mansion's owner.

The following recipes are from *The Blue Willow Inn Cookbook*:

Sweet Potato Soufflé

3 cups cooked fresh sweet
   potatoes, peeled if baked,
   drained if boiled
3 eggs
1 stick butter, melted
$\frac{1}{2}$ cup whole milk
$\frac{1}{4}$ cup light brown sugar

$\frac{1}{2}$ cup sugar
$\frac{1}{4}$ cup raisins (optional)
$\frac{1}{4}$ teaspoon cinnamon
1 teaspoon vanilla extract
Dash of nutmeg
1 cup miniature
   marshmallows

Preheat the oven to 350°. In a large bowl, mash sweet potatoes with a whisk or potato masher. Combine with eggs, butter, milk, brown and white sugars, raisins, if desired, cinnamon, vanilla, and nutmeg. Pour into a 9x13-inch casserole dish, and bake for 25 to 30 minutes. Top with marshmallows, and return to oven just long enough for marshmallows to melt.

Fried Green Tomatoes

2 eggs
$1\frac{1}{2}$ cups buttermilk
1 tablespoon plus $1\frac{1}{2}$ cups
   self-rising flour, divided
1 teaspoon salt, divided

1 teaspoon black pepper,
   divided
3 large green tomatoes,
   cut into $\frac{1}{4}$-inch slices
Vegetable oil for frying

In a bowl, mix together eggs and buttermilk. Whisk in 1 tablespoon flour, $\frac{1}{2}$ teaspoon salt, and $\frac{1}{2}$ teaspoon pepper. Soak tomato slices in this liquid. Whisk together remaining flour, salt, and pepper. Heat about 1 inch of oil to 350° in a heavy skillet. Dredge tomato slices, one at a time, in seasoned flour, shaking off any excess. Fry slices in hot oil; do not crowd. (Slices should not overlap as they cook.) Fry each side until it begins to turn brown. Turn in oil and fry until golden brown and crisp. Drain on paper towels. Salt to taste. Serve with Tomato Chutney. Makes 12 to 15 tomato slices.

TOMATO CHUTNEY:

1 (16-ounce) can whole
   tomatoes
1 cup light brown sugar
$\frac{1}{2}$ cup sugar
2 medium green peppers,
   finely chopped

1 medium onion, finely
   chopped
2 tablespoons ketchup
2 to 10 drops Tabasco
   sauce
1 teaspoon black pepper

In a heavy saucepan, stir together tomatoes, brown and white sugars, green peppers, onion, ketchup, Tabasco sauce, and pepper. Cook at a simmer for about 2 hours, stirring frequently until thickened. Cool. This will keep for 2 weeks in the refrigerator. Makes about 6 cups.

Chicken and Dumplings

1 (3- to 4-pound) chicken, disjointed	1 teaspoon salt
2 quarts plus ¼ cup water, divided	¼ cup shortening
	½ cup butter, melted
2 cups self-rising flour	2 teaspoons black pepper

Combine chicken and 2 quarts water in stockpot. Cook over medium-high heat until done, about one hour. Remove chicken from pot, reserving broth. Cool chicken in cold water. Remove bones, skin, and fat. Cut chicken meat into bite-size pieces. In a mixing bowl, combine flour and salt. Cut in shortening until mixture is coarse. Add remaining ¼ cup water, and mix well with your hands. Bring chicken broth back to a slow boil. With floured hands, pinch small quarter-size pieces of flour, and drop them into simmering chicken broth. Stir gently. Add butter and black pepper. Simmer 8 to 10 minutes. Slowly stir in chicken meat. Serve in soup bowls. Makes 8 to 10 servings.

Peach Cobbler

⅔ cup plus 2 tablespoons sugar, divided	1 (28-ounce) can sliced peaches
1 cup self-rising flour	
½ cup butter, melted, divided	

Preheat oven to 350°. In a bowl, coarsely mix ⅔ cup sugar, flour, and ¼ cup melted butter. Sprinkle about one-third of this mixture on the bottom of a baking dish. Add peaches and juice. Top peaches with remaining flour mixture. Sprinkle top with remaining 2 tablespoons sugar and remaining ¼ cup butter. Bake for 30 to 40 minutes, or until brown and bubbly. Serve hot. Makes 6 to 8 servings.

Note: If the juice from the peaches does not cover peaches, add a small amount of water just to cover the peaches. Too little liquid will make the cobbler dry. Too much liquid will make the cobbler soupy.

Blue Moon Café

40 East Main Street
Statesboro, GA 30458
(912) 489-1094

**Noel and Alicia Burnsed
Owners**

**Jason Scarborough
Executive Chef**

Blue Moon Café is the popular meeting place for folks in Statesboro. Located at 40 East Main Street, they are serving uptown dining in downtown Statesboro. There's nothing ordinary at the Blue Moon Café. From the eclectic décor to the gourmet food, the Blue Moon Café is the place to go for stylish dining. The atmosphere is romantic, yet laid back, with low lights, soothing jazz, and warm smiles. The dinner menu at the Blue Moon is seasonal and changes four times a year so that the executive chef, Jason Scarborough, can take advantage of the freshest, Bulloch County-grown produce. Blue Moon Café serves items as laid back as southern shrimp and grits and certified Angus filets, to unique, pallet-pleasing dishes such as Australian ostrich and local wild boar sausage. A dining experience such as this comes once in a Blue Moon.

Roasted Grouper

Sautéed mushroom and spring onion risotto with a balsamic browned butter sauce.

Salt and pepper
4 (6-ounce) grouper fillets
6 ounces extra virgin olive oil, divided
1 medium onion, finely chopped
1 clove garlic, crushed with salt to a purée
7 ounces risotto rice
1¾ pints vegetable stock
1 bunch spring onions, finely sliced

8 large shiitake caps, sliced
¼ cup heavy cream
½ cup grated Parmesan cheese
½ pound whole butter, softened
4 cups balsamic vinegar, reduced by half
1 cup corn syrup
Fresh thyme for garnish

Salt and pepper both sides of grouper. Heat 2 ounces of extra virgin olive oil in a nonstick, oven-safe pan. Sear grouper on one side until golden brown; turn and place in oven until albumin is forced out.

Heat 2 ounces olive oil in a large, heavy saucepan and add onion and garlic. Cook slowly, shaking the saucepan occasionally for about 5 minutes until onion and garlic are translucent. Add rice and continue to cook for 2 minutes, stirring at all times. Gradually add vegetable stock and cook slowly, stirring constantly, until the liquid is absorbed by the rice, about 15 minutes. In a separate saucepan, heat remaining 2 ounces oil and lightly sauté the spring onions and shiitakes with salt and pepper. Add to the risotto, along with heavy cream and Parmesan.

In a medium saucepan, add softened butter. Allow butter to brown for about 2 minutes. Then add corn syrup, stirring with a whisk, and continue to cook for an additional 2 minutes. Turn off heat, then slowly whisk in the reduced balsamic vinegar.

Serve in a medium-size bowl, adding risotto, grouper, and then the sauce. Finish with fresh thyme to garnish. Serves 4.

Hoisin Barbecue Shrimp

Lightly fire-grilled shrimp brushed with a local honey-soy hoisin, served over lime infused risotto.

HOISIN BARBECUE SAUCE:
2 tablespoons light sodium soy sauce
2 ounces good quality honey
4 ounces hoisin sauce

1 lime, juiced
2 cloves garlic, minced
1 pinch Chinese five-spice powder

Mix ingredients in a small bowl and allow to sit in refrigerator for at least 30 minutes.

20 large, fresh shrimp (5 per guest), peeled and butterflied
2 ounces extra virgin olive oil

20 ounces creamed fully cooked risotto, finished with the juice of one lime
1 bunch chives

Heat grill and lightly brush shrimp with extra virgin olive oil. Grill one side of the shrimp, then turn over and brush with Hoisin Barbecue Sauce, saving some of the sauce untouched. Once shrimp are fully cooked, place in a bowl and toss lightly with untouched sauce. Serve 5 shrimp over 5 ounces of lime risotto. Finish with finely chopped chives. Serves 4.

Historic Statesboro Inn

106 South Main Street
Statesboro, GA 30458
(912) 489-8628 • (800) 846-9466
www.statesboroinn.com

Michelle and Tony Gargas, Owners

The Historic Statesboro Inn is a 1904 Victorian oasis where porches, rockers, and tranquil garden ponds are blended with gracious southern hospitality. Our style is eclectic yet comfortable, with furnishings from three generations and a small pub with that European feel. Our sixteen rooms are a collection of all the amenities that you would expect, presented with the style and comfortable feeling of Grandma's home. Our cook brings all the traditional, southern foods back to the way you remember Grandma fixing a Sunday dinner. Our wide brick porches are the perfect place to have a glass of wine or perhaps a quick nap.

While you are at the Inn, plan to visit a garden display of native foliage at the Georgia Southern Botanical Garden, or see birds of prey and their habitats at the Ball Raptor Center. Enjoy a leisurely stroll to the downtown area where you can visit the restored 1894 Bulloch County Courthouse, the renovated 1905 Jaeckel Hotel once visited by the likes of William Jennings Bryan, Henry Ford Cornelius Vanderbilt, and Rotary founder Paul Harris, which now serves as Statesboro City Hall, or the newly renovated David H. Averitt Center for the Arts. Many interesting shops, restaurants, and antiques are always a treat in Statesboro.

Glazed Porterhouse Pork Chop

GLAZE:

3 cups water	Purée (recipe follows)
2 cups sugar	1 ounce liquid pectin

In a saucepan, bring water and sugar to a boil. Add Purée and pectin to water and reduce heat. Reduce to 2 cups and chill. The Glaze will thicken to half the consistency of jelly. To thicken, reheat and add pectin.

PURÉE:

1 habanero pepper	White pepper
1 large bell pepper	$\frac{1}{4}$ cup white distilled
1 teaspoon salt	vinegar, divided

Remove seeds from peppers and dice. Wear gloves when handling habanero peppers. Sauté in salt, white pepper, and $\frac{1}{2}$ of the vinegar until translucent. In a blender, pureé peppers with rest of the vinegar.

Marinate twelve-ounce porterhouse pork chops in some Glaze (overnight is best but an hour will do). Grill chops for 2 minutes on each side, turning with tongs. Place chops in oven-safe dish and baste with marinade. Bake at 400° for about 15 minutes or until internal temperature reaches 160°.

Tip: Use the remaining Glaze for fish, chicken, or pork.

Beer Cheese Spread

1 cup grated Cheddar
  cheese
½ cup goat cheese
1 ounce light beer
1 tablespoon Worcestershire
  sauce

1 teaspoon dry mustard
Dash of salt and pepper
Stone-ground wheat
  crackers

Combine all ingredients except crackers in a food processor and blend until smooth. Chill and serve with stone-ground wheat crackers.

Paper Bag Apple Pie

1 (9-inch) pastry shell
1¼ cup sugar, divided
2 tablespoons plus ¾ cup
  flour, divided
½ teaspoon nutmeg
1 teaspoon cinnamon

5 to 6 large baking apples
  (about 2½ pounds,
  peeled and sliced)
2 tablespoons lemon juice
½ cup butter

Prepare one 9-inch pastry shell. Preheat oven to 425°. Mix ½ cup sugar, 2 tablespoons flour, nutmeg, and cinnamon and toss with apples to thoroughly cover. Put in shell and drizzle with lemon juice. Mix ¾ cup sugar, ¾ cup flour, and butter until about the size of peas. (Do not overmix.) Sprinkle on top of pie and place in a heavy brown paper bag large enough to cover pie loosely. Fold up open end and fasten with staples or paper clips. (In this age of plastic bags, parchment paper will work as well.) Place on a cookie sheet or other pan to collect any overflowing juices. Bake for 1 hour or until apples are tender and top is golden. When opening make slits in bag to allow steam to escape, then remove pie. Serve warm with a scoop of ice cream.

Blueberry Pecan Bread Pudding

The Statesboro Inn serves this for breakfast with fresh fruit and bacon or sausage.

3 tablespoons butter
¾ to 1 loaf French or
  Italian bread
1 cup fresh or frozen
  blueberries
½ cup grated white
  chocolate

1 cup chopped pecans
6 eggs
1 cup sugar
1 teaspoon cinnamon
2 tablespoons vanilla
5 cups milk

Melt butter and use to prepare a 9x13-inch pan. Cube ¾ to 1 loaf of French or Italian bread—enough to cover the bottom of the pan. Spread blueberries, chocolate, and pecans over bread. Combine eggs, sugar, cinnamon, vanilla, and milk and pour over the rest. At this point, you can cover and refrigerate the pan, or you can cover and bake at 350° for about 45 minutes. (If you refrigerate, you will need to cook a little longer.) Uncover for the last 15 minutes. It is done when the top is brown and the mixture is puffed. Serve warm with a scoop of ice cream or a vanilla bourbon sauce.

Variations: You can substitute any fresh or frozen berries, sliced apples, and sliced peaches.

Leigh Ann's Café

609 Brannen Street
Statesboro, GA 30458
(912) 764-7858

Michael and Leigh Price, Owners

Leigh Ann's Café, est. 2001, is a quaint, locally owned restaurant. Chef Michael Price, and wife Leigh, welcome each day with the chance to prepare new and exciting dishes to please any palate. Michael, from Italian heritage, grew up cooking with his grandmother preparing homemade native dishes. He knew at an early age that cooking would one day become his full-time job. Leigh, born and raised in rural Bulloch County, never dreamed of owning a restaurant. Although around food in a different manner, Leigh grew up as a farmer's daughter.

"Food with flair" describes all of Chef Michael's original recipes. Taking pride that the food is always fresh and the presentation is at its finest, Leigh Ann's serves dishes with true southern hospitality.

Lunch consists of over 50 original wraps. "Fine Dining in a Casual Atmosphere" is the motto for dinner. White crisp tablecloths and linen napkins cover the tables, soft piano music fills the background, and wine is served from various regions around the world. Leigh Ann's offers many delicacies indigenous to the area such as Low Country Shrimp and Grits, Crab Cakes, fresh seafood, and more. Chef Michael also creates regional dishes such as quail, duck, and veal. He prepares homemade desserts on a daily basis topped with fruits native to Georgia.

Fried Green Tomatoes with Remoulade

2 medium green tomatoes
1 tablespoon salt
1 tablespoon fresh-cracked black pepper
2 cups panko (Japanese bread crumbs)
2 tablespoons paprika
1 cup chopped fresh parsley
4 eggs
2 cups all-purpose flour
2 cups vegetable oil

Slice tomatoes and sprinkle with salt and pepper. Combine bread crumbs, paprika, parsley, salt and pepper. Crack eggs in separate bowl, flour in another. First, dip tomato into flour, shaking off excess—this is very important. Next, dip into egg, letting the excess drip off. Press tomato into bread crumbs, thoroughly coating both sides. Heat oil in skillet. When oil is hot, add tomatoes, frying on medium heat. Cook until golden on both sides. Drain on paper towels. Drizzle with Remoulade and serve with a fresh lemon slice. Serves 8.

REMOULADE:
¼ cup ketchup
1 cup mayonnaise
¼ cup chopped fresh parsley
2 teaspoons hot pepper sauce
1 medium shallot
2 tablespoons capers
2 teaspoons vinegar
1 tablespoon paprika
2 teaspoons lemon juice

Combine all ingredients in food processor. Blend until smooth. Refrigerate for 2 hours.

Roasted Bone-In Pork Chop with a Sweet Vidalia Onion Pan Gravy

2 teaspoons olive oil
3 tablespoons butter, divided
Salt and pepper to taste
2 (8-ounce) pork chops
½ cup chopped Vidalia onion
¼ cup fresh chives (chopped)
1 tablespoon all-purpose flour
½ cup whole milk
Fresh parsley for garnish

Preheat oven to 350°. In a frying pan on medium heat, add olive oil and 1 tablespoon butter. Salt and pepper both sides of pork chops. When oil and butter are hot, lay chops in pan and sear for 1 minute, then turn over. Place in oven for 7 minutes. Flip the chops and return to the oven for another 7 minutes. Pull chops from oven and set aside.

Using the same pan that the pork chops were cooked in, melt remaining butter over medium heat. Scraping bottom of the pan, add onions and chives. Salt and pepper to taste. After caramelizing for 45 seconds, add flour and incorporate. Reduce heat and add milk, whisking until well blended. When sauce begins to thicken, remove from heat. Place the pork chops on a plate and pour the pan gravy over. Top with fresh parsley. Serves 2.

Georgia Peach with Smirnoff White Chocolate Peach Mousse

4 medium-ripe peaches
1 lemon
1 pound white chocolate
3 (3-ounce) packs cream cheese, softened
2 tablespoons Smirnoff Peach Vodka
1¼ cups sugar, divided
2 cups heavy cream
4 sprigs fresh mint

Cut tops off peaches using a paring knife. Hollow out and reserve for later. Rub peach with lemon juice on inside and on the top piece. Place covered in refrigerator.

Cut chocolate into small squares and melt using a double boiler. Meanwhile, combine cream cheese, vodka, and ½ cup sugar in mixing bowl. Mix thoroughly. When chocolate has melted, add to cream cheese mixture. Mix completely and chill. In a separate bowl, whisk together heavy cream and ½ cup sugar. Whisk vigorously until soft peaks rise. Fold whipped cream in with chocolate mix. Chill for 1 hour.

In food processor, combine peaches (from coring out the peach from earlier) and remaining sugar. Blend until smooth. Strain and chill. Using a pastry bag, pipe mousse into peaches. Replace top of peach and push one sprig of mint into top to act as a leaf. Drizzle peach sauce around sides and serve.

Monroe residence

Steeplechase Grille & Tavern

306 East Second Street
Vidalia, GA 30474
(912) 537-7900

James (Sam) L. Owens
Chef/Owner

Cream of Vidalia Onion Soup

2 quarts Vidalia onions, diced	2 quarts chicken stock
9 ounces margarine, divided	2 tablespoons ham base
	$^3/_4$ cup flour
1$^1/_2$ teaspoons black pepper	2 cups half-and-half

In a stockpot, sauté onions and 3 ounces margarine until they become transparent. Add black pepper and stir until completely mixed. Add chicken stock and ham base, stirring to combine. Heat mixture until it begins to boil. Meanwhile, make a roux with remaining 6 ounces margarine and flour. Once stock begins to boil, add the roux, combining thoroughly. Continue cooking soup until it begins to thicken and returns to a boil. At this point, slowly add half-and-half while stirring until completely incorporated; remove from heat. Garnish with grated Jack and Cheddar cheese and chopped Vidalia spring onions. Yields 1 gallon.

Note: Roux needs to be at room temperature before adding to a hot soup. Adding hot roux to hot soup can cause to soup to break down. Place roux in cooler or freezer, if necessary, to cool it down before adding to a soup.

Vidalia Onion Cheese Dip

3 cups diced Vidalia onions	2$^1/_2$ cups mayonnaise
1 pound Swiss/American cheese, grated	1 teaspoon garlic salt

Mix all ingredients and pour into a greased baking dish. Bake in a preheated 350° oven for 35 to 40 minutes until lightly brown. Serve with corn chips. Yields 8 cups.

Cajun Chicken Pasta

1 (8-ounce) boneless, skinless chicken breast	$^1/_2$ cup ($^1/_4$-inch julienne) Vidalia onion strips
Blackening seasoning as needed	$^1/_2$ cup carrot coins
1 tablespoon olive oil	3 fluid ounces Spicy Black Bean Sauce (recipe follows)
1 cup broccoli florets	
$^1/_2$ cup ($^1/_4$-inch julienne) red bell pepper strips	4 ounces vermicelli noodles, cooked

Grill a chicken breast that has been liberally seasoned on both sides with blackening spice. When done, dice into $^1/_4$-inch pieces. Set aside. Meanwhile, place olive oil in skillet over high heat. Add vegetables and sauté until vegetables lose their raw appearance. Remove from heat and add Spicy Black Bean Sauce. Next, add hot noodles to vegetables and black bean sauce and toss to coat. Serve in a pasta bowl. Place chicken on top of noodles and serve. Yields half order.

SPICY BLACK BEAN SAUCE:

$^1/_4$ cup oil	1$^1/_2$ tablespoons chile oil (pepper oil)
$^1/_4$ cup finely chopped fresh garlic	2 cups soy sauce
$^1/_4$ cup finely chopped fresh ginger	$^1/_2$ cup canned black beans, rinsed under cold water
1 cup $^1/_4$-inch diced Vidalia onions	1 tablespoon red pepper flakes
$^1/_4$ cup seasoned rice wine vinegar	1 cup water

Heat oil in a skillet. Add garlic, ginger, and onions and sauté until onions no longer look raw. Add remaining ingredients and bring to a boil. Reduce heat, then simmer for 5 minutes. Yields 3$^1/_2$ cups.

The Coast Region

$\mathcal{B}$eaches, tidal marshlands, swamps, historic districts, and abundant fresh seafood…you're in the Coast Region. Georgia's oldest city, Savannah, is home to more than fifty historic inns and bed and breakfasts, the third oldest Jewish synagogue in America, twenty-one public squares, and the Savannah Music Festival's fifteen-day ode to music which brings jazz, blues, rock, gospel, and international beats. The small barrier island of Tybee Island is located 20 minutes east of downtown Savannah. Here you'll find live music, three-miles of beach, a 1773 lighthouse, a museum, Fort Screven, and Fort Pulaski. On St. Simons Island the restored St. Simons lighthouse remains a navigational aid and houses a museum featuring exhibits on the history of the lighthouses and the Golden Isles. Don't forget to fill up on some local seafood.

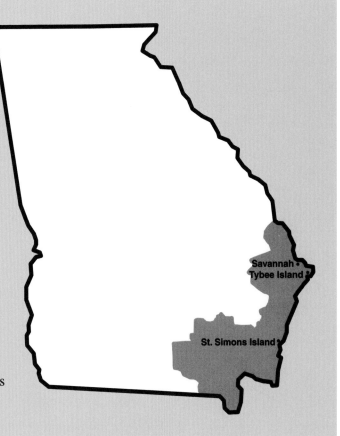

The Coast Region Menu

The Coast Region Menu

Alligator Soul Restaurant

"Fine Southern Cuisine"

114 Barnard Street
Savannah, GA 31401
(912) 232-7899 or (912) 232-8038

Alligator Soul Restaurant in Savannah is the third southern cuisine restaurant for owners Hilary and Maureen Craig.

Hilary Craig (Hilbo to his friends) is a native Floridian who was raised with the help of a Creole woman who exposed him at a young age to this extraordinary culinary world of flavors and textures. He opened his first Alligator Soul in Everett, Washington, in 1995, and again in Seattle, Washington, in 1998.

His Seattle restaurant was awarded one of the "Top Ten" restaurants in Seattle in 1998, seven months after opening, no small feat in a city commonly known for culinary sophistication. His flagship restaurant in Everett has been awarded Best Restaurant Outside Seattle, in Puget Sound by *Seattle Magazine*.

Somewhere along the way, Chef Craig created five sauces and spice blends: Georgia Peach Hot Sauce, Creole Belle Hot Sauce, Gator Rub, Chipotle Mayo, and Barefoot Barbecue. Three of his condiments won first place at the Texas Fiery Food Show in Austin, Texas, on his first try. His Chipotle Mayo won him first place in both the condiment category and the mayo category.

Crawfish Spring Rolls with Red Pepper Glaze

FILLING:

1 small carrot, peeled and julienne	1 pound crawfish tailmeat
1 red pepper, finely julienne	$\frac{1}{4}$ cup soy sauce
1 small cabbage, finely chiffonade	$\frac{1}{4}$ cup sesame oil
	1 tablespoon grated ginger
1 cup bean sprouts	1 tablespoon minced garlic
1 red onion, sliced paper thin	Creole seasoning and salt to taste
$\frac{1}{4}$ cup chopped cilantro	1 package spring roll wraps

Add first 12 ingredients into a bowl and let sit overnight.

Place spring roll wrappers in front of you with point facing you like a diamond. Place Filling $\frac{1}{3}$ of the way up the wrapper. Fold bottom point over filling. Fold the 2 sides in and roll up. Use a little water to seal the last point. Place on tray and dust with cornstarch.

RED PEPPER GLAZE:

2 red bell peppers	Sugar
Vinegar	

Dice up red peppers and purée in food processor. Measure purée in a measuring cup and put in a nonreactive pot. For every cup of purée, add $\frac{1}{2}$ cup of vinegar and 2 cups sugar. Bring to a boil, cooking over low heat for 20 minutes. Set aside to cool.

Fry spring rolls in a deep-fryer or heavy saucepan with peanut oil at 375° until golden brown. Drain on paper towels. Cut on a bias and serve with Red Pepper Glaze drizzled over top.

Chocolate Bread Pudding with Wild Turkey Ice Cream

FILLING:

6 eggs	4 cups half-and-half
½ cup sugar	1 loaf French bread, cut
1 teaspoon vanilla extract	into small cubes
10 ounces white chocolate, melted	

Combine eggs, sugar, vanilla, and melted white chocolate until well incorporated. Add half-and-half and bread cubes. Let sit for 2 hours until bread has absorbed all liquid. Spoon into well-buttered, 2-ounce ramekins. Cook in 350° oven for 15 to 20 minutes until golden brown on top. Let cool to room temperature and remove from ramekins.

WILD TURKEY ICE CREAM:

1½ cups sugar	1 vanilla bean
10 yolks	2 ounces Wild Turkey
1 quart half-and-half	bourbon

Whisk sugar into yolks until pale yellow. Heat half-and-half in saucepan. Add ¼ of the hot half-and-half to yolk mixture and whisk. Add remaining yolk mixture and vanilla bean back into half-and-half and continue cooking over low heat until thick. Cool in refrigerator for at least 6 hours.

Remove vanilla bean. Pour into ice cream maker along with Wild Turkey. Make ice cream.

Roasted pecans   **Powdered sugar**

To serve, reheat Chocolate Bread Pudding in oven. Spoon a scoop of Wild Turkey Ice Cream on top of bread pudding and sprinkle with roasted pecans and powdered sugar.

Stuffed Georgia Quail with Wild Mushroom Bread Pudding

STUFFING:

1 pound bacon, diced	5 sprigs marjoram,
1 pound bulk sausage	cleaned and chopped
3 to 4 cups bread crumbs	3 egg whites

Cook bacon until done but not crispy. Remove from pan. Add bulk sausage to pan; crumble and cook until done. Combine sausage, bacon, bread crumbs, and marjoram in a bowl. Taste for seasoning and adjust, if necessary. Add egg whites to moisten.

WILD MUSHROOM BREAD PUDDING:

4 ounces wild mushrooms	1 teaspoon Creole spice
½ teaspoon minced garlic	2 cups half-and-half
1 tablespoon oil	4 large eggs, beaten
Salt and pepper to taste	3 cups diced French bread
1 chicken bouillon cube, crushed	

Sauté mushrooms and garlic in oil. Season with salt, pepper, bouillon, and Creole spice. Add half-and-half, eggs, and bread. Let stand until bread soaks up all liquid. Bake in 4-ounce ramekins at 350° for approximately 20 minutes. Allow to cool at room temperature. Finish cooling in refrigerator.

8 semi-boneless quail   **Caul fat (optional)**

Stuff each quail with Stuffing to look like little baseballs. Cross legs and toothpick them into the breast. Encase them in caul fat (or brush with butter) and roast at 400° for 10 to 15 minutes, until interior temperature is 140°. (Remember Stuffing is already cooked). Add Bread Pudding the last 2 to 3 minutes to warm up.

PINOT NOIR GRAPE REDUCTION:

2 tablespoons chopped shallots	1 cup veal glacé
1 teaspoon garlic	2 cups chopped, seedless grapes
2 cups Pinot Noir	

Sauté shallots and garlic. Add wine and reduce by half. Add veal glacé. Add grapes and cook until grapes are soft. Adjust seasoning. Spoon Pinot Noir Grape Reduction onto 4 plates and add 2 quail to each plate. Add warmed Bread Pudding. Serve with asparagus or another vegetable.

Belford's of Savannah
Casual Fine Dining in City Market

315 W. St. Julian Street
Savannah, GA 31401
(912) 233-2626

George E. Denmark II
Executive Chef

Belford's She-Crab Soup

¹⁄₂ pound butter	1 cup crab stock
¹⁄₄ cup finely diced onion	1 quart heavy cream
¹⁄₄ cup finely diced red pepper	1 quart half-and-half
¹⁄₄ cup finely diced peeled carrot	¹⁄₂ cup dry sherry
¹⁄₄ cup finely diced celery	1 (6-ounce) can tomato paste
¹⁄₂ cup all-purpose flour	1 pound crab claw meat, cleaned

In a heavy-bottom pot, slowly melt butter. When butter is melted, add onion, pepper, carrot, and celery. Cook until onions are clear. When onions are ready, slowly incorporate all the flour to make a fairly thick roux. Cook roux about 15 to 20 minutes on a low flame, but do not brown. After roux has cooked, increase temperature to a medium flame. Then add crab stock to the pot, allowing stock to thicken before adding cream. When stock is incorporated, start adding heavy cream, allowing it to thicken before adding next ingredient. Continue this process with half-and-half also.

When dairy products have been incorporated, and soup has thickened slightly, reduce heat to low and allow soup to simmer for at least one hour. (It is very important to keep the heat low under this soup as it is very easily scorched, and should never be allowed to come to a boil.) Just before removing from heat, add sherry, tomato paste, and crabmeat. Let soup heat back up to 165° and remove from stove. This recipe makes approximately 8 servings.

Grouper Provençal Belford's

TAPENADE:

¹⁄₂ cup stuffed green olives	2 teaspoons chopped garlic
¹⁄₄ cup capers	3 anchovy fillets
¹⁄₂ teaspoon crushed red pepper	1 teaspoon lemon juice

Preheat oven to 350°. In a food processor, incorporate olives, capers, red pepper, garlic, anchovies, and lemon juice, using the pulse button until the Tapenade has a course texture. Do not purée the Tapenade into a paste.

Salt and pepper to taste	Olive oil
Tomatoes, sliced	16-20 asparagus spears, steamed
4 (8-ounce) black grouper fillets	¹⁄₄ cup chopped parsley
8 tablespoons panko (or Japanese style) bread crumbs	

On a nonstick baking pan, arrange half of the tomatoes 2x2 and lightly salt and pepper them. On top of each pair of tomatoes place 1 grouper fillet. Rub 1 tablespoon of Tapenade on each grouper fillet. Place remaining tomato slices 2x2 on top of grouper fillets. Then top each fillet with about 2 tablespoons bread crumbs and lightly drizzle with olive oil. Place in oven for 15 to 18 minutes.

To arrange the plate, fan 4 to 5 asparagus spears from the center of the plate. Place the grouper on the asparagus in the center of the plate. Drizzle entire plate with olive oil and garnish with the chopped parsley.

Belford's Spinach Salad

1 large onion	3 pounds fresh baby
½ teaspoon sugar	spinach, washed
1 cup sliced mushrooms,	and spun dry
sautéed in clarified	½ teaspoon sugar
butter	Bleu cheese dressing
6 strips cooked bacon, cut	Bleu cheese crumbles
into thin strips	Sugared walnuts

Start by peeling the onion and slicing it into rings. Then sauté onion rings in a small pan with sugar until they are a light brown color. Keep onions, mushrooms, and bacon warm until time to serve the salad.

In a large mixing bowl, add spinach and bleu cheese dressing and toss together. The dressing should not be too heavy; it should just coat the spinach leaves. Now arrange the spinach onto 6 chilled salad plates. Garnish with onion, mushrooms, bacon, bleu cheese crumbs, and sugared walnuts. Serves 6.

Belford's Shrimp, Greens, and Grits

GREENS:

1 quart water	Dash Tabasco sauce
1 ham hock	Salt and pepper to taste
2 tablespoons white	2 bunches collard greens,
vinegar	washed, cleaned, and cut

In a large pot, add water, ham hock, vinegar, Tabasco sauce, salt and pepper. Bring to a boil. Cook ham hock for about an hour on medium heat, then add collard greens. Cook greens for about 30 minutes. Adjust salt to taste.

GRITS:

1 cup grits	3 cups chicken stock
¼ teaspoon salt	

In a heavy saucepan, slowly stir grits and salt into briskly boiling chicken stock. Reduce heat to medium low; cover. Cook 5 to 7 minutes or until thickened, stirring occasionally. Remove from heat. Pour grits out onto a cookie sheet and spread them out evenly. Put into refrigerator for at least 2 hours.

Once grits have set, cut into small triangles. Dust grit cakes with seasoned flour and deep-fry for about 5 minutes.

SHRIMP:

28 jumbo shrimp	4 ounces diced green
6 ounces cooked bacon,	onions
diced	4 ounces diced tomatoes
8 ounces white wine	4 ounces shredded
4 ounces whole butter, cut	Parmesan cheese
into cubes	

In a large sauté pan, sauté shrimp and bacon until shrimp are almost done. Add white wine and allow it to reduce by half. When wine has reduced, mount sauce with whole butter and remove from heat.

On 4 large plates, arrange collard greens, then add grit cakes on top of greens. Arrange shrimp around grits and greens, and pour sauce over shrimp and grit cakes. Garnish with green onions, diced tomatoes, and Parmesan cheese.

Bistro Savannah

309 W. Congress Street
Savannah, GA 31401
(912) 233-6266
www.dininggroupsouth.com/Bistro

**Tracy Lemmonds
Chef**

Smoked Jalapeño and Green Tomato Salsa

Best if made one day ahead.

2 garlic cloves, minced	1 cup chopped cilantro
6 smoked jalapeños, peeled and diced with seeds	¼ cup olive oil
	¼ cup lime juice
3 pounds green tomatoes, diced and seeded	2 tablespoons sherry vinegar
1 cup diced red onions	Salt and pepper

Combine all ingredients, adding salt and pepper to taste. Chill. Serve with chips or any white fish. Yields 1 quart.

Low Country Crab Cakes

1 cup fresh corn kernels	1 tablespoon Texas Pete Hot Sauce
½ cup diced red peppers	
½ cup diced green onions	1 pound fresh lump crabmeat
2 eggs	
¼ cup Dijon mustard	2 cups crushed Ritz Crackers
½ cup mayonnaise	
1 tablespoon Worcestershire sauce	Japanese bread crumbs
	Salt and pepper to taste

Lightly sauté vegetables and set aside. In a mixing bowl, combine eggs, mustard, mayonnaise, Worcestershire sauce, and hot sauce. Add cooled sautéed vegetables. Lightly fold in crabmeat, trying not to break up the lumps. Add cracker crumbs, leaving the mix still moist. Divide into cakes. Coat with Japanese bread crumbs and sauté over medium heat for 4 minutes on each side. Serve with Red Pepper Remoulade. Makes 6 to 8 cakes.

RED PEPPER REMOULADE:

1 cup mayonnaise	2 tablespoons capers
½ cup roasted red pepper fillets, cleaned and puréed	¼ cup diced bread and butter pickles
1 tablespoon lemon juice	2 teaspoons Old Bay Seasoning
¼ cup minced onions	

Combine mayonnaise, red pepper purée, and lemon juice. Add onions, capers, and pickles. Add Old Bay Seasoning and taste. (Add until taste suits you.) Yields 2 cups.

Mercer House, Savannah

Boar's Head Grill and Tavern

"Casual fine dining, in an old cotton warehouse, overlooking the Savannah River."

1 North Lincoln Street Ramp
Savannah, GA 31401
(912) 651-9660

Philip and Charlene Branan, Owners

In *Romantic Days and Nights in Savannah* (©2001), Georgia Byrd cites the Boar's Head as "Savannah's most romantic restaurant!" Boar's Head was the first restaurant on Riverstreet and has been in operation since 1959.

Chocolate Bread Pudding

Awarded First Prize in Dessert Category at Taste of Savannah 2004!

Diced croissants	1 vanilla bean, split
6 ounces sugar	8 whole eggs
Pinch salt	1 pound semisweet
1 quart heavy cream	chocolate, chopped

Prepare six (6-ounce) custard cups by buttering and dusting with sugar. Divide diced croissant evenly between the cups.

In a heavy-bottom pot, combine sugar, salt, cream, and vanilla bean. Scald mixture but do not boil. Lightly whip eggs in a bowl, then whip in half the cream mixture. Temper this back into remaining cream. Remove vanilla bean. Scrape pulp and add it to the custard. Add the chocolate and stir until it is completely melted. Fill each custard cup with the mixture, working the croissants with your fingers, making sure that they are completely saturated. Bake in a water bath at 325° until the custard is fully set (about 45 minutes). To serve, run a knife around each cup and invert onto plates. Serve with hard sauce. Serves 6.

Shrimp and Sausage Stew

2 pounds large shrimp, peeled and deveined	½ pound ripe tomato, chopped
Olive oil	2 tablespoons chopped fresh basil
1 pound andouille sausage, sliced	16 ounces shrimp stock
1 small red onion, chopped	Tabasco sauce to taste
4 garlic cloves, minced	1 teaspoon Worcestershire sauce
8 ounces beer (Bud works just fine)	4 tablespoons whole butter, cut into pieces
2 pieces summer squash, sliced	Fried grit cakes or rice pilaf
½ pound fresh okra, sliced	

Sauté shrimp for 2 minutes in a little olive oil. Add sausage and cook together for 1 minute. Add the onion and garlic; cook 1 minute more, then deglaze pan with beer. Bring to a boil, then add vegetables and basil. Pour in the shrimp stock, cover, and cook for 3 minutes. Season with Tabasco sauce and Worcestershire sauce. Swirl in whole butter; taste and adjust seasonings, if necessary. Serve in large bowls with fried grits cakes or rice pilaf. Serves 4.

Elizabeth on 37th

105 East 37th Street
Savannah, GA 31401
(912) 236-5547

Michael and Elizabeth Terry
Owners

Elizabeth on 37th, in Savannah, Georgia, opened in May of 1981 as the creation of Chef Elizabeth Terry and her husband Michael. Elizabeth is devoted to classic southern cooking and has extensively researched Savannah cooking of the 18th and 19th centuries. Elizabeth's reputation as an innovator and leader in the cuisine of the "New South" is well established. She has combined traditional cooking methods with an avid interest in fresh, health-conscious menus.

Guests pass fragrant herb gardens as they enter the large southern mansion that houses Elizabeth on 37th. Built in 1900, the lavish Greek Revival style home features a spacious dining room with beautiful architectural details, decorated in a palette of historic Savannah colors and patterns.

Now, this architectural gem is the setting for a fine dining experience complete with award-winning southern cuisine, top shelf spirits, and a carefully chosen wine list.

Bluffton Oysters with Pernod Cream Sauce in Pastry

2 tablespoons butter
¼ cup minced country ham or prosciutto
2 tablespoons Pernod
2 tablespoons flour
1 cup heavy cream
1 tablespoon minced thyme, stem discarded
2 cups quartered, sliced green Vidalia onions
2 pints small Bluffton oysters, drained well
6 individual baked pastry shells
1 tablespoon minced fresh tarragon

In a large skillet over high heat, melt the butter. Add the country ham and sauté until brown. Pour in Pernod and stir; add flour and whisk for 1 minute to cook. Whisk in heavy cream and the thyme and simmer while whisking until thick. The sauce may be made ahead to this point and set aside to cool, then refrigerated.

In a large skillet over high heat, sauté onions and oysters for 1 minute. Reheat the sauce in a small sauté pan. Combine onions, oysters, and sauce. Heap mixture into prepared shells. Sprinkle with fresh tarragon and serve immediately.

Forsyth Park Savannah

Potato Crusted Red Snapper

5 Idaho potatoes, peeled and grated
$\frac{1}{2}$ cup butter, melted
1 tablespoon salt
$\frac{3}{4}$ tablespoon freshly ground black pepper
1 cup freshly grated Asiago cheese (Parmesan may be substituted)
1 tablespoon finely minced lemon zest
6 (6-ounce) red snapper fillets

Preheat oven to 425°. Bring a large pot of lightly salted water to boil; add grated potatoes and boil for 30 seconds, then drain. Plunge into an ice bath and drain immediately. Spread potatoes on a plate or baking sheet to dry. Toss with melted butter, salt, pepper, cheese, and lemon zest. Lightly coat each fish fillet with potato, pressing potato with fingertips.

Place the potato crusted fish on a lightly oiled baking sheet and roast fish for 15 to 20 minutes in the oven until lightly browned and cooked through. Yields 6 servings. Serve with Brussels Sprouts Hash.

BRUSSELS SPROUTS HASH:

3 cups quartered Brussels sprouts, core removed
$\frac{1}{2}$ cup $\frac{1}{4}$-inch diced Vidalia onions
2 cups chopped crookneck squash, cut in half and soft seed center discarded and outer part cut into $\frac{1}{2}$-inch dice
$\frac{1}{4}$ cup cooked and chopped bacon
1 cup heavy cream
$\frac{1}{2}$ cup rich chicken stock, degreased
Fresh-cracked black pepper to taste

Place all ingredients in large sauté pan and cover. Cook over high heat and bring just to a boil. Remove lid and continue to cook over high heat until all liquid is completely reduced and vegetables are tender, approximately 7 to 10 minutes. Stir and season to taste with cracked pepper. Serves 4 to 6.

Peach Blueberry Pie

CRUMB TOPPING:

$\frac{2}{3}$ cup all-purpose flour
$\frac{1}{4}$ teaspoon ground ginger
$\frac{1}{3}$ cup light brown sugar
4 tablespoons ($\frac{1}{2}$ stick) chilled unsalted butter, diced

Place all ingredients in bowl of mixer with paddle attachment. Process until mixture resembles coarse meal. Remove to a small bowl and refrigerate.

FILLING:

6 peaches peeled, sliced, divided
2 tablespoons cornstarch
3 tablespoons quick cooking tapioca
1 cup sugar
$\frac{1}{2}$ teaspoon cinnamon
1 tablespoon lemon juice
1 cup fresh blueberries
1 (9-inch) pie crust, chilled

Preheat oven to 375°. Combine 1 cup peaches, cornstarch, tapioca, sugar, cinnamon, and lemon juice in a medium saucepan over high heat. Bring to a boil and cook, while stirring until thick and shiny, about 3 minutes. Cool 10 minutes, then stir in rest of peaches and berries and spoon into chilled pie shell. Crumble on the topping and bake in the middle of the oven for 50 minutes until fruit bubbles and topping is brown. Place a sheet pan on the shelf below the pie to catch any dripping juice. Cool before cutting. Serves 6.

IL Pasticcio

2 East Broughton Street
Savannah, GA 31401
(912) 231-8888

**Pino Venetico
Proprietor**

Funghi All'Indivia
(Appetizer)

10 ounces walnuts,
    chopped, divided
4 egg yolks
1 shot glass of champagne
    vinegar
Salt and cracked black
    pepper to taste
½ pint extra virgin olive oil

4 medium-size portobello
    mushrooms
Shot of white wine
4 heads endive
1 whole red pepper,
    roasted, chopped

In a food processor, purée 5 ounces walnuts, egg yolks, vinegar, salt and pepper, slowly adding oil until thick. Bake remaining 5 ounces chopped walnuts for 5 minutes at 400°. Place mushrooms on a sheet pan, bottom side up. Drizzle with oil, white wine, salt and pepper. Bake at 400° for 30 minutes. After baking, remove and julienne mushrooms. On each plate, serve 1 fanned mushroom over endive. Top with vinaigrette and toasted walnuts. Garnish with chopped red pepper.

Trota Farcita
(Entrée)

2 medium eggplants,
    peeled and diced
½ stalk celery, chopped
1 carrot, chopped
½ onion, chopped
3 Roma tomatoes, diced
1 small handful dried
    cherries

1 shot glass of extra virgin
    olive oil
1 glass red wine
2 ounces sugar
½ glass red wine vinegar
4 cleaned trout, with skins
Salt and pepper to taste
Fresh parsley, chopped

Preheat oven to 450°. Deep-fry eggplant to light brown. Strain and dry on paper towels. In a saucepan over high heat, sauté celery, carrot, onion, tomatoes, and cherries in oil. Cook for several minutes until soft. Add red wine, sugar, and vinegar. Reduce a bit, then add eggplant. Stir and reduce until mixture becomes like a stuffing. Lay trout on a sheet pan, opened with skins down. Bake until trout is white. On side of each fillet, spoon stuffing and close with other half. Add salt and pepper to taste. Bake another 2 minutes. Plate and sprinkle with parsley. Pair with a favorite starch and vegetable. Il Pasticcio recommends jasmine rice seasoned with saffron and asparagus sautéed with garlic oil. Yields 4 servings.

Statue of Florence Martus, Savannah's Waving Girl

Risotto ai Porcini
(Entrée)

4 ounces dried porcini
 mushrooms
5 handfuls riso Arborio
1 garlic clove, chopped
1 gallon vegetable broth,
 divided
Salt and cracked pepper
 to taste

Fresh chopped parsley
1/2 pound Parmigiano
 Reggiano, grated,
 divided
2 rounded tablespoons of
 floured butter

One half hour before cooking, soak mushrooms in a pint of warm water. In saucepan over medium heat, add riso, garlic, porcini mushrooms (including water), one quart vegetable stock, salt, pepper, and some parsley. When water begins to reduce, add another quart of vegetable stock and stir. Repeat this until all stock is used. When riso doubles and mixture thickens, remove from heat. Add 2/3 Parmigiano and butter. Cover and let stand for 5 minutes. Stir and plate. Sprinkle with remaining Parmigiano and parsley.

Tiramisù
(Dessert)

Tiramisù is best when prepared a day in advance.

5 egg yolks
6 ounces sugar
1 pound mascarpone
 cheese
1 egg white, whipped

1 cup white rum*
36 ladyfingers
12 cups coffee
1/4 cup powdered cocoa

In a mixing bowl, beat egg yolks with sugar until frothy. Stir in cheese and mix carefully. Add whipped egg white, then the liqueur. Mix well into a smooth cream. In a baking dish, spread a layer of cream. Quickly soak ladyfingers in coffee, turning on both sides. Add another layer of cream and soaked ladyfingers. Top with remaining cream and spread evenly with a spatula. Using a sifter, top with a generous amount of cocoa powder. Refrigerate for 2 hours and serve.

*Can substitute Triple Sec, Grand Marnier, or sweet Marsala wine for rum.

Johnny Harris Restaurant, Inc.

1651 East Victory Drive
Savannah, GA 31404
(912) 354-7810

Norman L. Heidt
President and General Manager

Johnny Harris Restaurant was established in 1924. Today it's not all that different from the one your parents and grandparents went to. It offers thick steaks and prime rib, seafood, and the most savory bar-b-que in coastal Georgia. The Johnny Harris Onion Blossom is the first and best in Savannah and the Brunswick Stew is incomparable. Johnny Harris' Bar-B-Que and Ribs have been voted Best in the City and the Bar-B-Que Sauce was selected #1 by *Food & Wine Magazine* and tied for first in *Cooks Magazine*. *Real Bar-B-Que* named Johnny Harris' sauce one of the nation's best. Johnny Harris was featured on the Food Network's *Food Finds* and is listed in *Mobil Guide* and *AAA*.

Jamie Carver
Executive Chef

Chef Carver is a 1991 graduate of the American Culinary Federation. He competed in the Culinary Olympics in 1994 and won a silver and bronze medal. In 1995, he won a gold medal in the U.S. Chefs Open. He was voted Best Chef in Atlanta in 1996. Chef Carver owned a catering business before moving to Savannah in 2003 to join the Johnny Harris organization. He has a 30-minute cooking show on Savannah television.

Shrimp and Scallops Salad

Salt and pepper
Shrimp and scallops (as many as you like)
2 teaspoons oil
Assorted lettuce (any kind you like)
12 black olives, sliced
5 cherry tomatoes, sliced
$\frac{1}{4}$ cup julienne-cut cucumbers
$\frac{1}{2}$ cup vinaigrette dressing
$\frac{1}{2}$ cup freshly grated Parmesan cheese (or more)

Salt and pepper shrimp and scallops. Heat oil. Sauté shrimp and scallops for 2 minutes on each side. Remove from skillet. Chill for 7 minutes.

In a bowl, add lettuce, olives, tomatoes, and cucumbers. Add seafood. Add dressing and toss. Serve in a chilled bowl. Sprinkle with Parmesan cheese.

Chicken Marsala

2 chicken breasts, butterflied
Salt and pepper to taste
All-purpose flour
2 tablespoons oil
$\frac{1}{4}$ cup chopped red onion
$\frac{1}{4}$ cup sliced mushrooms
$\frac{1}{2}$ cup diced yellow squash
$\frac{1}{2}$ cup diced green bell pepper
$\frac{1}{4}$ teaspoon minced garlic
$\frac{1}{4}$ cup Marsala wine
$\frac{1}{4}$ cup heavy cream
Pasta or mashed potatoes

Season both sides of chicken with salt and pepper. Flour chicken. Heat oil in skillet. Add chicken; cook until light brown. Turn chicken over. Add onion, mushrooms, squash, and bell peppers. Cook for 2 minutes. Add garlic. Remove from stove, add Marsala wine, and ignite. Add cream and allow it to reduce by half. Serve over pasta or mashed potatoes. Serves 2.

BBQ Salmon

4 tablespoons oil
2 salmon fillets, butterflied
Salt and pepper to taste
$\frac{1}{4}$ cup sliced red and green bell peppers
$\frac{1}{4}$ cup olives
White wine
$\frac{1}{4}$ cup barbecue sauce (preferably Johnny Harris brand)
Cooked rice or pasta

Heat oil in skillet. Salt and pepper salmon. Add peppers and olives. Deglaze with white wine. Add barbecue sauce. Add cooked rice or pasta. Serves 2.

Shrimp and Pasta with Ham

8 scallops
8 medium shrimp
Salt and pepper to taste
2 tablespoons olive oil
$\frac{1}{2}$ cup diced ham or tasso
1 lemon, juiced
$\frac{1}{2}$ cup white wine
$\frac{1}{4}$ teaspoon minced garlic
2 cups cooked pasta (bowtie, angel hair, or your favorite)
$\frac{1}{2}$ cup grated fresh Parmesan cheese

Season scallops and shrimp with salt and pepper. Heat oil in skillet. Add scallops and shrimp; cook 1$\frac{1}{2}$ minutes on each side. Add ham. Add lemon juice and white wine. Add garlic and pasta. Cook until pasta is hot. Add cheese. Allow to melt, and serve. Serves 4.

Classic Rainbow Trout

$\frac{1}{4}$ cup oil
Salt and pepper
2 rainbow trout (classic is served head on)
$\frac{1}{4}$ cup flour
2 lemons
$\frac{1}{4}$ cup white wine
$\frac{1}{4}$ cup diced yellow onions
2 tablespoons whole unmelted butter

Heat oil. Salt and pepper both sides of trout. Lightly flour the trout. Add to pan, skin side down. Cook both sides of trout. Add fresh-squeezed lemon juice. Add white wine and onions. Allow to reduce by half. Add butter, but do not allow butter to melt all the way. Place on plate, skin side down. Serves 2.

Bananas Savannah

(Chef's twist on Bananas Foster)

2 tablespoons whole butter
2 bananas, sliced
$\frac{1}{2}$ cup brown sugar
$\frac{1}{4}$ to $\frac{1}{2}$ cup Southern Comfort (your choice)
$\frac{1}{4}$ cup heavy cream
Your favorite ice cream or pound cake

Heat butter. Add bananas and cook for 3 minutes. Add brown sugar and allow to melt. Remove from heat and add whiskey. Allow to flame. Add heavy cream. Serve hot over ice cream or pound cake. Serves 2.

The Lady & Sons

102 W. Congress Street
Savannah, GA 31401
(912) 233-2600
www.ladyandsons.com

Paula H. Deen
Owner and Proprietor

For a most enjoyable meal choose from the award-winning buffet or southern gourmet menu. The Lady & Sons was voted *USA Today's* 1999 Meal of the Year. Look for Paula every Saturday morning at 10:30 a.m. on the Food Network. The accolades keep pouring in for The Lady & Sons: Georgia Small Business of the Year and National Small Business Person of the Year 2nd Runner-up! Don't miss The Lady & Son's new retail shop featuring southern spices, cookbooks, and cheese biscuit and hoe cake mixes.

Swiss Steak

1 round steak* (approximately 1½ pounds)	2 garlic cloves, crushed
	1 (14½-ounce) can diced tomatoes
1 teaspoon garlic powder	1 medium onion, cut into strips
Salt and pepper to taste	
All-purpose flour for dusting	1 medium bell pepper, cut into strips
⅓ cup vegetable oil	Water

Cut steak into serving-size pieces. Season to taste with garlic powder, salt and pepper. Dust meat with flour. In heavy skillet, brown both sides of meat in vegetable oil. Transfer to Dutch oven. Combine garlic, tomatoes, onion, bell pepper, and 1 tomato-can measure of water. Pour over steak and simmer until meat is tender. Season to taste with salt and pepper. Serves 4.

*To ensure tenderness, it is necessary to have the butcher run the round steak through a cuber.

Hint: This is good to cook in a Crock-Pot on LOW for a most fabulous dinner.

Recipe from The Lady & Sons Savannah Country Cookbook *published by Random House ©1997*

Madison Square, Savannah

Farmer's Pork Chops

8 medium potatoes
½ medium onion
Salt and pepper to taste
White Sauce (recipe
follows; or you may also
use your own)

1 cup all-purpose flour
2 tablespoons Lawry's
Seasoned Salt
8 center-cut pork chops,
about ½ inch thick
⅓ cup vegetable oil

Preheat oven to 350°. Peel potatoes; slice ¼ inch thick and cover with cold water. Slice onion into very thin slices. Cut slices in half. Drain potatoes; layer half the potatoes in a well-greased 10x15-inch casserole dish. Sprinkle with salt and pepper to taste. Scatter half of onion slices on top of potatoes. Repeat with remaining potatoes and onions. Cover potatoes with White Sauce. Cover casserole dish with plastic wrap and microwave for 5 minutes on HIGH or bake uncovered for 15 minutes.

Mix together flour and seasoned salt and dredge pork chops in flour mixture. Lightly brown chops in vegetable oil. Do not cook them completely. As chops are removed from frying pan, lay them on top of potatoes. Bake at 350° for 45 to 60 minutes. The juices from the pork chops will drip down into the potatoes. Delicious! Serves 8.

WHITE SAUCE:

8 tablespoons (1 stick)
butter
½ cup all-purpose flour
1 to 2 teaspoons salt
½ to ¾ teaspoon pepper

4 cups milk
¼ cup chopped fresh
parsley or chives
(optional)

Melt butter; remove from heat. Stir in flour; add salt and pepper. Return to heat and cook, stirring constantly, until mixture is bubbly. Add milk, 1 cup at a time. Bring to a boil over medium heat, stirring frequently. Reduce heat and simmer 1 to 2 minutes, then let stand at least 1 to 2 minutes. Stir in parsley or chives, if desired.

Recipe from The Lady & Sons Savannah Country Cookbook *published by Random House ©1997*

Turnip Greens with Cornmeal Dumplings

¾ pound smoked meat
(smoked turkey wings
are excellent)
4 quarts water
1 teaspoon House
Seasoning (recipe follows)
2 chicken bouillon cubes
¼ teaspoon ground ginger

1 bunch turnip greens
with roots
4 tablespoons (½ stick)
butter
1 teaspoon sugar
(optional: may be used
if greens are bitter)

Place smoked meat in water along with House Seasoning, bouillon, and ginger. Cook over low heat for 1½ hours.

Strip turnip leaves free of the big stem that runs down the center of each leaf. Wash in a sink full of clean water. Drain and wash twice more, since greens can often be sandy. Peel and slice or quarter roots. Add greens to meat; cook for another 30 minutes, stirring often. Add roots and continue to cook for approximately 15 minutes or until roots are tender. (Reserve ⅔ cup liquid after cooking, if making dumplings.) Add butter and dumplings, if desired and serve. Serves 4 to 6.

HOUSE SEASONING:

1 cup salt
¼ cup black pepper

¼ cup garlic powder

Mix well and store in a shaker.

CORNMEAL DUMPLINGS:

1 cup all-purpose
cornmeal
½ teaspoon salt
1 small onion, chopped

1 egg
⅔ cup liquid from
cooked turnips

Mix all ingredients together. Dipping by teaspoonfuls, gently roll batter in the palms of your hands into approximately 1-inch balls; drop into boiling turnip liquid. Make sure each dumpling is completely covered in liquid by shaking the pot gently; do not stir. Boil for about 10 minutes.

Recipe from The Lady & Sons Savannah Country Cookbook *published by Random House ©1997*

Grandgirl's Fresh Apple Cake from Georgia

CAKE:

2 cups sugar	1 tablespoon cinnamon
3 eggs	1 tablespoon vanilla
1½ cups vegetable oil	extract
¼ cup orange juice	3 cups peeled and finely
3 cups all-purpose flour	chopped apples
1 teaspoon baking soda	1 cup shredded coconut
1 teaspoon salt	1 cup chopped pecans

Preheat oven to 325°. Generously grease a tube pan. Combine all ingredients in a large bowl in the order given and mix well. Pour batter into prepared pan and bake for 1½ hours. Shortly before Cake is done, make the Sauce.

SAUCE:

½ cup (1 stick) butter	½ cup buttermilk
1 cup sugar	½ teaspoon baking soda

Melt butter in a large saucepan; stir in sugar, buttermilk, and baking soda, and bring to a good rolling boil, stirring constantly. Boil for 1 minute. Pour Sauce over hot Cake (in the pan) as soon as you remove it from the oven. Let stand 1 hour, then turn out. Serves 16 to 20.

Recipe from The Lady & Sons, Too *published by Random House ©2000*

Mrs. Wilkes's Boarding House

107 West Jones Street
Savannah, GA 31401
(912) 232-5997

Margie Martin, Proprietor

The following recipes are from *Mrs. Wilkes's Boardinghouse Cookbook.*

Fried Chicken

2 tablespoons evaporated milk	All-purpose flour
2 tablespoons water	Vegetable oil
1 (2½-pound) fryer, cut up and sprinkled with salt and pepper	

Pour evaporated milk and water over chicken, and marinate about 10 minutes. Dip chicken in bowl of all-purpose flour. Shake off excess flour. Deep-fry in vegetable oil at 300°, or pan-fry on medium heat (making sure oil is hot before putting chicken in). Make sure chicken is covered with oil at all times. Fry until golden brown. (Same recipe may be used for pork chops.)

Cheese Grits

1 cup grits	4 cups water
¼ cup butter	2 egg yolks, beaten well
1 (6-ounce) package garlic cheese	2 egg whites, beaten stiff
	Cracker or dry bread
1 teaspoon salt	crumbs

Cook grits, butter, and cheese in salted water until well done. Add egg yolks. Fold in egg whites. Put in greased casserole. Sprinkle top with crumbs. Bake at 350° for 45 minutes. Serves 6 to 8. (Sharp cheese may be substituted for garlic cheese.)

Georgia Pecan Mist Cake

12 egg whites	12 egg yolks
½ teaspoon salt	3 cups pecans (chopped
3½ cups powdered sugar	fine)

Beat whites and salt until foamy. Gradually add sugar and continue to beat until stiff but not dry. Beat yolks until thick; fold into whites. Gently fold in pecans. Bake in tube pan at 350° for 50 minutes. Freezes well.

Chicken and Dumplings

1 (2½-pound) chicken,	1 teaspoon salt
cut up, ready to cook	1 teaspoon pepper

Place chicken in a saucepan and cover with water. Sprinkle with salt and pepper. Boil over medium heat for 30 minutes. Pour off broth and save for Dumplings.

DUMPLINGS:

2 cups all-purpose flour	½ cup water
2 cups milk, divided	Salt and pepper to taste

Mix flour, ½ cup milk, and water in a bowl, and knead until dough is firm. Mash flat on a floured surface. Let stand for 10 minutes. Roll out with a rolling pan until knife-blade thin, and cut into 2-inch squares. Drop into boiling broth. Cook for 10 minutes over high heat. Reduce heat to low and return chicken to pot. Pour remaining 1½ cups milk into mixture, and stir. Remove from heat. Serve with salt and pepper to taste.

Savannah Red Rice

2 medium onions, diced	1 cup tomato sauce or
2 medium bell peppers,	catsup
diced	½ teaspoon Tabasco sauce
Bacon drippings	4 strips bacon, fried crisp
2 cups cooked rice	and crumbled
6 to 8 tomatoes, chopped	Salt and pepper to taste
and cooked	2 tablespoons grated
1 (16-ounce) can tomatoes	Parmesan cheese

Preheat oven to 325°. Brown onions and peppers in bacon drippings. In a large bowl, combine rice, onions, peppers, tomatoes, tomato sauce, Tabasco sauce, and bacon. Season with salt and pepper to taste. Mix well. Pour into greased casserole pan and sprinkle cheese on top. Bake for 30 minutes or until rice is dry enough to separate. Serves 4 to 6.

Note: You may also add 1 pound of cooked shrimp, sausage, pork, or ham.

Wilkes Boarding House, Savannah

Sapphire Grill

110 St. Julian Street
Savannah, GA 31401
(912) 443-9962
www.sapphiregrill.com

**Christopher Nason
Chef and Proprietor**

Chef Nason's extensive training began when he was cooking in suburban Philadelphia kitchens while attending Lehigh University. He relocated to Charleston, South Carolina, where he studied at Johnson and Wales University. Prior to opening Sapphire Grill, Chris was chef at the DiRoNa award-winning Village Café in Charleston, South Carolina, chef at Anson, also in Charleston, and executive chef at Bistro Savannah. Chef Nason opened Sapphire Grill in Savannah in January, 1998.

The Sapphire Grill is conveniently located in Savannah's City Market. The menu features a wide variety of seafood, lamb, veal, and beef dishes along with sumptuous nightly specials. The chef concentrates on the culinary seasons with his menu, and the items available change with fresh frequency, using the best in fresh truffles, mushrooms, eastern seaboard fish and meats, and organic produce.

Southern Living magazine had these comments: "It's indeed Savannah's most exciting eatery, and we'd go back again and again" and "Chef and owner Christopher Nason offers an incredible dining experience." *Bon Appetit* magazine said, "This is the place to go for a comfortable good time while dining on excellent steaks, seasonal cooking, and sensational seafood appetizers."

Spicy Lemon Curd

3 to 4 tablespoons Meyer lemon zest
1/2 cup fresh Meyer lemon juice
1/2 jalapeño pepper, seeded and diced very small
1 1/2 cups sugar
6 tablespoons butter
3 eggs, lightly beaten

In a medium saucepan over medium-high heat, combine zest, lemon juice, jalapeño pepper, and sugar. Bring to a boil; reduce heat to medium low and simmer for 5 minutes. Add butter and stir until it has melted. Remove from heat and cool to room temperature. Beat eggs into cooled lemon juice mixture until well blended. Return to heat and cook over medium low heat, stirring constantly 10 to 15 minutes until it thickens to coat back of spoon. Remove from heat. Store in refrigerator.

Mango Honey

1/2 tub honey
1 cup dark rum
2 whole peeled shallots
Zest of 1 lemon
2 sprigs rosemary
1 mango, peeled, pitted, and chopped

Add all ingredients to saucepan and cook at low heat for 30 minutes. (Do not burn!)

Watermelon Peppercorn Sorbet

1 cup sugar
2 cups water
2 cinnamon sticks
2 tablespoons crushed coriander seeds
2 pounds watermelon (weighed without seeds)
1/2 tablespoon cracked black pepper
1 tablespoon freshly chopped mint
3 tablespoons fresh lemon juice

In copper saucepan, dissolve sugar in water. Add cinnamon sticks and coriander seeds and boil for 5 minutes. Cover and let infuse in refrigerator until cold. Purée watermelon and add pepper and mint. Strain syrup into watermelon purée and stir in lemon juice. Add mixture to ice cream maker and run for 45 minutes. Put in freezer until firm.

17Hundred90

307 E. President Street
Savannah, GA 31401
(912) 236-7122

Eddie Williams, General Manager
Brian Benthnol, Executive Chef
Amaine S. Adams, Sous Chef

17Hundred90 is Savannah's only inn with a full service restaurant and lounge, and is consistently rated by tourists and food magazines as one of Savannah's finest restaurants. 17Hundred90 has been a gourmet tradition in Savannah for over a century and has been acclaimed as "the most elegant restaurant in Savannah" by *Gourmet Magazine*.

Mediterranean Potato Cake

3 pounds potatoes, peeled and cubed	¾ tablespoon Dijon mustard
6 anchovies	1 tablespoon herbs de Provence
¼ cup capers	
⅓ cup chopped pepperoncini peppers	3 ounces butter
	5 ounces heavy cream
¼ cup pitted and chopped niçoise olives	3 eggs, beaten
⅛ cup minced roasted garlic	Salt and pepper to taste

Peel and cut potatoes; boil in pot of salted water and cover until tender, then drain and allow to steam off and dry. In a bowl, slightly crush potatoes with a spoon or by hand. Add all ingredients except butter, cream, and eggs to the potatoes. Adjust seasonings. Fold in first the eggs, then butter, and finally the cream. Shape into 12 potato cakes and chill until ready to serve. Gently fry in hot oil until golden on both sides. Serves 12.

Chocolate Bombe with Raspberry Sauce

6 to 7 cups chocolate chips	1 cup espresso
1 cup sugar	6 whole eggs
1 cup espresso powder	6 egg yolks
1 pound butter	

Using a double boiler with moderate heat, combine and melt chocolate chips, sugar, espresso powder, and butter. When the first 4 ingredients are melted, temper in the eggs slowly over the heat (so as not to scramble the eggs). Line a cake pan with tin foil. Spray tin with nonstick spray and pour in mixture. Allow to cook until the top looks a bit cracked; the cake will not be "set" yet. Allow to rest for 15 minutes. Put in freezer overnight. Makes 1 (9-inch) cake.

RASPBERRY SAUCE:

3 cups raspberries	1 cup water
2 cups sugar	

Heat above ingredients and reduce until thick. Let cool. Serve over chocolate cake.

Crab Bisque

½ pound butter	2 tablespoons crab base
½ pound all-purpose flour	1 pound lump blue crabmeat
½ quart heavy cream	
3 quarts water	Salt and white pepper to taste
1½ cups sherry	
½ gallon milk	

Make a blonde roux with butter and flour. Stir slowly and do not burn. Add in remainder of ingredients, in order listed. Blend mixture together. Cook until a creamy consistency is achieved. Season with salt and white pepper. Serves 12.

Halyards Restaurant Group

600 Sea Island Road, Suite 19
St. Simons Island, GA 31522
(912) 638-9100
www.halyardsrestaurant.com

Dave Snyder, Executive Chef

Lobster and Avocado Salad with Plantains, Cilantro, and Almond-Lime Vinaigrette

ALMOND-LIME VINAIGRETTE:

4 limes, juiced	5 ounces almond oil
5 ounces blended olive oil	Salt and pepper to taste

Combine lime juice and oils. Season with salt and pepper.

SALAD:

1 pound Maine lobster, cooked, cleaned, and diced	15 whole almonds
	Cilantro, julienne
	Salt and pepper to taste
2 ounces baby greens, washed and dried	10 plantains, 1/8 inch sliced, fried
1 shallot, minced	
1/2 tomato, skinned and julienned	

Combine all ingredients except plantains with Vinaigrette. Garnish with fried plantains.

Seared Diver Sea Scallops and Pork Belly

(Over Spring Onions, Favas, and Licorice-Scented Mushroom Broth)

PORK BELLY:

1 pound pork belly, trimmed	Black pepper
	Ground coriander
Kosher salt	

Rinse pork well. Lightly season with spices. Braise in stock for 6 to 7 hours, or until tender, at 325°. Cool and cut into portions.

SCALLOPS:

Scallops (find those that haven't been chemically treated)	Salt and pepper to taste
	Blended olive oil
	1 teaspoon unsalted butter

Season scallops with salt and pepper. Sear in hot pan in blended oil for 10 seconds; then lower heat to medium. Add butter; continue on low for 20 seconds. Turn over and cook about 30 seconds. (May need to cook more or less depending on size of scallops.)

MUSHROOM BROTH:

1/2 pound crimini mushrooms, quartered	1 tablespoon porcini powder
1/4 pound portobellos, sliced	1 quart chicken stock, strained well
Blended olive oil	2 ounces soy sauce
2 shallots, sliced	1 sprig thyme
4 garlic cloves, pounded	1 bay leaf
4 ounces leek green, sliced and rinsed	

Sear mushrooms in very hot oil. Sear in small quantities to ensure mushrooms will caramelize. Add shallots, garlic, and leek. Turn heat to medium and simmer for 5 minutes. Stir in powder and cook for 30 seconds. Add stock, soy, and herbs. Cook for 30 minutes. Strain.

Georges' of Tybee

1105 E. Highway 80
Tybee Island, GA 31328
(912) 786-9730
robertwood@georgesoftybee.com

Robert Wood, Chef

Seared Scallops in Velvet Corn Sauce

VELVET CORN SAUCE:

6 ears corn, kernels cut off cob	1 tablespoon chopped fresh thyme
1 large shallot, sliced	¾ cup white wine
1 tablespoon minced garlic	½ cup cream
Olive oil	½ pound butter, cut into chunks
1 sprig sage	Salt and pepper to taste

Add first 3 items to stainless steel sauce pot with olive oil and sauté quickly for 3 to 4 minutes. Add herbs and wine, and reduce by ⅔; add cream, reduce by half. Transfer to blender; purée while adding butter one piece at a time. Finish with salt and pepper and chinois purée.

18 (U-10) scallops	10 basil leaves (chiffonade at last minute)
Salt and pepper to taste	
5 ounces fresh chèvre (I use Sweetgrass Dairy)	

Season scallops with salt and pepper and sear on both sides in a cast-iron skillet. Ladle 1 ounce Velvet Corn Sauce onto plate and spread out to cover the plate. Place 3 scallops in center of plate; crumble ¾ ounce of chèvre and sprinkle along with basil over scallops and sauce. Makes 6 appetizers.

Black Grouper Encrusted with Sunflower Seeds and Accented by Pomegranate-Plum Reduction

POMEGRANATE-PLUM REDUCTION:

8 pomegranates	¼ stick cinnamon in cheese cloth
4 plums	
1 tablespoon butter	3 cardamom pods
1 cup port wine	½ lemon
1 spike clove	Pinch of salt

Juice pomegranate through a food mill; sauté plums in butter, then add port wine and spices. Reduce by half, then add pomegranate juice; reduce by half, then pull out spices and squeeze. Purée remaining ingredients and season with lemon and a pinch of salt. Chinois purée and taste again; set aside until needed.

SUNFLOWER SEED CRUST:

¾ cup sunflower seed	1 tablespoon salt
½ cup all-purpose flour	Pinch cayenne

Toast sunflower seeds in oven for about 7 minutes at 350°. Pulse in food processor with remaining ingredients.

6 (8-ounce) black grouper fillets

Salt fillets and lay in Sunflower Seed Crust. Press firmly on the fillets; flip and repeat. Sauté over medium heat until golden brown on one side; flip and finish cooking in a 400° oven. It will take about 4 minutes per inch of thickness of the fish.

Spoon Pomegranate-Plum Reduction onto 6 plates and add encrusted fillet to each plate. Serve with basmati or white rice with sautéed green beans or chayote squash.

Lighthouse, Tybee Island

Hunter House

1701 Butler Avenue
Tybee Island, GA 31328
(912) 786-7515
www.hunterhouseinn.com

John L. Hunter, Owner
Espy Geissler, Chef/Co-owner

Built in 1910 as a family beach house, Hunter House was renovated in 1998 and is now one of the best restaurants and inns on the Georgia coast.

Its southern beach house charm begins to embrace you as you climb up the stairs to the second floor verandah. Entering the dark wood-paneled foyer is only the beginning of a special evening of Victorian ambiance and culinary delights. There you are greeted by John Hunter and his friendly staff before being seated at a candle-lit table in one of the three small dining rooms.

Different specials are prepared each night featuring fresh seafood and excellent meats. The appetizers range from rich seafood bisque to Cuban black bean soup. While the meals of local black grouper, Atlantic salmon or yellowfin tuna are delicious, the "pot roast dinner" continues to be a favorite year after year.

The bar offers a varied selection of wines from different countries, which can be enjoyed with your meal or after dinner on the porch in a rocking chair.

The Inn has four rooms ranging from a large suite with a fireplace to smaller one bedroom and bath—all within walking distance to several breakfast restaurants.

A visit to Tybee Island is a unique experience, but a meal at Hunter House makes it unforgettable.

Roasted Chilean Sea Bass with Pernod Scented Lemon Cucumber Cream and Grilled Asparagus over Boursin Cheese Garlic Chive Mashed Potatoes

2 to 3 pounds large russet potatoes, peeled and quartered
2 ounces ($\frac{1}{2}$ stick) unsalted butter
4 tablespoons soft Boursin cheese
3 tablespoons chopped garlic chives or regular chives
Buttermilk
Salt and pepper to taste
$\frac{3}{4}$ cup mayonnaise
$\frac{1}{4}$ cup heavy cream
$1\frac{1}{2}$ teaspoons Pernod (anise-flavored liqueur)
$1\frac{1}{2}$ teaspoons fresh lemon juice
$2\frac{1}{2}$ teaspoons tomato paste
$\frac{1}{2}$ hot house cucumber, peeled, seeded, and diced $\frac{1}{4}$ inch
4 (6- to 8-ounce) Chilean sea bass fillets (or halibut, flounder, or sole)
$\frac{1}{4}$ cup extra virgin olive oil with squeeze of lemon
Paprika to taste
1 pound asparagus, tough ends removed
Lemon wheels
Scallions

Preheat oven to 425°. Peel and chop potatoes; add to salted boiling water to cover. Cook until soft. Drain water; add butter and let melt. Mash potatoes until somewhat smooth. Beat in Boursin cheese and garlic chives, and stir in buttermilk until soft. Add salt and pepper to taste and keep warm.

In a food processor, combine mayonnaise, cream, Pernod, lemon juice, and tomato paste for 2 minutes. Add salt to taste. Add diced cucumber; pulse to mix. Set aside.

Coat a sheet pan with nonstick spray and arrange fillets on pan. Brush with oil and lemon juice mixture, and season with salt; place in middle of oven. Roast approximately 6 to 8 minutes, depending on thickness of fish. Remove and cover with foil to keep warm.

Preheat a heavy skillet with grid over medium-high heat. Coat asparagus with lemon oil mix, salt and pepper. Cook until marked on 2 sides and just done. Remove from pan and keep warm.

Place 1 cup of potatoes in each of the 4 plates, then place sea bass on potatoes. Drizzle lemon oil mix around fish and potatoes. Pour 2 tablespoons of sauce on fish. Dust with paprika. Top with 3 asparagus, a lemon wheel, and sliced scallions.

The Southern Rivers Region

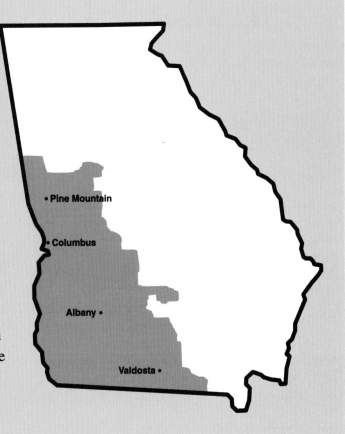

From roses and azaleas, to peanuts and presidents, the Old South is alive and well in the Southern Rivers Region. Columbus preserves its rich heritage through the Coca-Cola Space Science Center, Columbus Museum, Columbus Museum Uptown, and Springer Opera House. Albany is the cultural center of the region with a symphonic orchestra, theater group, and ballet company, and is also the birthplace of Ray Charles. Pine Mountain is the site of Franklin D. Roosevelt's Little White House State Historic Site. For more presidential history, visit the Jimmy Carter National Historic Site and Boyhood Farm in Plains. If it's football season, Valdosta is the place to be on Friday night where you can watch the winningest high school football team in the nation. Go Wildcats!

The Southern Rivers Region Menu

Harvest Moon Restaurant

230 W. Broad Street
Albany, GA 31701
(229) 439-7077

Bo Henry, Owner

Chicken Alfredo Lasagna

1 tablespoon butter
2 teaspoons minced garlic
1 quart heavy cream
1 cup grated Parmesan cheese
1 teaspoon Italian seasoning
Salt and pepper to taste
1 pound mozzarella cheese
4 (6-ounce) chicken breasts, grilled and diced
4 (8x10-inch) precooked lasagna sheets

Heat on high, the butter, garlic, and heavy cream in a pot and bring it to a boil. Immediately add grated Parmesan, turn heat down, and stir with a wire whisk. Keep sauce on medium heat and add seasonings, until desired taste and thickness.

Place 1 lasagna sheet in a nonstick, deep baking pan. Spread Alfredo over sheet, add 1 diced, grilled chicken breast, and cover with mozzarella. Place another sheet on top and repeat process for each layer. Cover with foil and bake at 400° for about 30 minutes, or until edges start to brown. Serves 4 to 6.

Bruschetta Dip

10 to 12 Roma tomatoes, diced small
2 cups sliced black olives
2 cups diced red onions
1 cup chopped fresh basil
1 cup feta cheese crumbles

Combine and mix all ingredients, by hand, to form a dip. Serve over toasted garlic bread. Serves 4 to 6.

Roasted Eggplant Dip

4 large eggplants
6 Roma tomatoes, diced
$\frac{1}{2}$ cup shredded Parmesan cheese
$\frac{1}{2}$ cup crumbled feta cheese
3 stalks green onions, diced

Cut eggplants in half lengthwise and place on nonstick baking sheet. Bake for approximately 30 minutes at 450°, or until they are soft to touch. Let cool. In a medium-size container, add tomatoes, Parmesan cheese, feta, and green onions. Remove eggplant fillings from skin, by scooping with spoon or hand. Chop up and add to other mixture. Toss and mix all ingredients. Serve with toasted garlic bread or chips. Serves 4 to 6.

Mama Ludie's Fried Chicken

This is Bo's grandmother's recipe!

Remove skin from chicken pieces. Wash really well. Place chicken in dish and cover with milk. Let chicken rest for an hour or more. Drain milk. Salt and pepper the chicken. Coat heavily with flour. Deep-fry in hot grease.

Mom's Vegetable Soup

1 to $1\frac{1}{2}$ pounds lean beef stew meat
6 to 8 cups water
2 ($10\frac{3}{4}$-ounce) cans tomato soup
2 (16-ounce) cans diced tomatoes
1 (16-ounce) can cut green beans (undrained)
1 (16-ounce) can whole-kernel corn (drained)
1 cup chopped carrots
$1\frac{1}{2}$ cups sliced/chopped celery
1 large or 2 medium onions, sliced
3 to 4 cups diced potatoes

Boil beef in large stockpot covered in 6 to 8 cups of water for 45 minutes. Save stock. Take out meat and remove any fat or gristle. Cut into bite-size pieces. Add all other ingredients to the stock. Salt and pepper to taste. Bring to a boil. Reduce heat. Simmer on low heat with the soup having a slight bubble for at least 2 hours. Makes a big pot. Freezes really well.

Recipes from Bo's mother, Ruth Henry

Squash Casserole

1½ cups squash	3 tablespoons onion

Combine squash and onions and cook until tender.

1 cup grated Cheddar cheese	1 egg
	½ cup milk
1 cup cubed bread crumbs (small cubes)	3 tablespoons butter

Mix ingredients and add to cooked squash. Bake uncovered at 350° for 35 to 40 minutes.

Recipes from Bo's mother, Ruth Henry

Pecan Pound Cake

½ pound butter	½ pint sour cream
3 cups sugar	1 teaspoon vanilla
6 egg yolks	6 egg whites, beaten
3 cups cake flour	¾ cup chopped pecans
¼ teaspoon baking soda	

Cream butter and sugar. Add egg yolks one at a time, beating after each addition. Sift together the cake flour and baking soda. Add to butter mixture. Add sour cream and vanilla and blend until smooth. Fold in softly beaten egg whites and chopped pecans to mixture. Pour into a greased tube pan or 2 loaf pans and bake at 300° for 1 hour and 30 minutes.

Recipes from Bo's mother, Ruth Henry

Mom's Peanut Butter Pie

8 ounces cream cheese	9 ounces Cool Whip topping
⅔ cup crunchy peanut butter	
	1 large or 2 small graham cracker crusts
2 cups 4x (superfine) sugar	
1 cup milk	

Combine cream cheese with crunchy peanut butter until smooth. Mix together sugar and milk. Add to above ingredients. Stir in Cool Whip topping. Put in 1 large or 2 small graham cracker crusts. Freeze.

Recipes from Bo's mother, Ruth Henry

Miriam's Café & Gallery

1350 13th Street
Columbus, GA 31901
(706) 327-0707

Faye Simmons, Owner

Miriam's House Salad

MIRIAM'S STYLE PECANS:

½ pound butter (1 stick)	½ cup honey
½ cup pancake syrup	2 pounds pecans

Melt butter in skillet. Mix in syrup and honey. Toss in pecans and coat. Cook for 2 to 3 minutes (the pecans will burn fast, so stir continuously). Spread pecan mixture on a tray or large baking pan and cook at 350° in oven for 5 or 6 minutes until toasted. Allow time for cooling. Store at room temperature; do not store in refrigerator.

MIRIAM'S CITRUS SALAD DRESSING:

½ cup Mandarin orange juice	1 cup concentrated orange juice
½ cup champagne vinegar	1 cup olive oil
	Pinch fresh cilantro
½ cup Coco Lopez (cream of coconut)	Pinch fresh basil

Mix all ingredients in blender and blend until smooth.

California Greens (spring mix)	Cherry tomatoes
	Endives for garnish
Whole Mandarin orange sections (canned)	

Toss well the greens, pecans, oranges, tomatoes, and dressing. Garnish with endives.

Miriam's Tomato Parmesan Soup

1 onion, chopped	Salt and pepper to taste
1 clove garlic (may put less), minced	Pinch fresh basil (optional)
Cooking oil (very little)	Pinch dry thyme (optional)
½ cup white wine	1 to 2 pints heavy cream
2 (#10) cans (6 quarts) whole tomatoes	Parmesan cheese to taste
Cornstarch (optional)	Salt and pepper to taste

Sauté onions and garlic in saucepan with a very small amount of oil. When it begins browning, add white wine. Cook off the liquid. Add 2 (#10) cans of whole tomatoes and cook off the liquid. If needed, add a little cornstarch to thicken. Blend in blender and add salt, pepper, basil, and thyme to taste. Add 1 to 2 pints of heavy cream to desired consistency. Add fresh Parmesan cheese (do not cook long or the cheese will brown and burn).

Miriam's Flour Tortilla Chips

1 to 2 packages flour tortillas (can be plain or mixed variety)	Peanut oil
	Cayenne pepper to taste
	Kosher salt to taste

Cut tortillas into 3 or 4 strips. Add peanut oil to deep-fryer at 350° heat. Fry tortilla strips for 2 to 3 minutes until golden brown. Drain. Sprinkle with cayenne pepper and kosher salt.

Miriam's Stuffed Chicken

6 ounces double chicken breast	Pepperidge Farms Italian bread crumbs
2 egg whites	1 ounce Boursin cheese
¼ cup water	2 to 3 Spanish olives with pimentos
Japanese bread crumbs (or Pepperidge Farms croutons, crushed)	Flour
	Peanut Oil

Cover chicken with plastic wrap and pound flat; remove wrap. In bowl, mix egg whites and water and whip. In another bowl, combine equal amounts of Japanese bread crumbs and Italian bread crumbs. Add Boursin cheese and olives to flattened chicken. Fold chicken over. Dust with flour. Dip chicken into egg wash, then coat with bread crumbs. Deep-fry in peanut oil for 5 to 6 minutes until golden brown. Remove from oil and place in baking pan and bake in 350° oven for 10 to 15 minutes.

Miriam's Squash Casserole

2 pounds zucchini and squash (remove seeds and chop)	Kosher salt and pepper to taste
Large white onion	Pinch basil
½ teaspoon fresh-minced garlic	Pinch thyme
5 to 6 strips Applewood Smoked Bacon	Pinch cilantro
3 cups half-and-half	1 cup shredded mozzarella and Cheddar cheeses
6 fresh eggs	2 cups bread crumbs

Cut all seeds out of squash and chop. Sauté squash, onion, and garlic with diced bacon. In a bowl, combine half-and-half, eggs, salt, pepper, herbs, and cheese. Sprinkle in bread crumbs and mix in sautéed vegetables. Put in baking dish and bake at 350° for 25 to 30 minutes.

Tavern Off Broadway

14 Eleventh Street
Columbus, GA 31901
(706) 324-2238

Ian Halley
General Manager

Crab Cakes with Pineapple Salsa

5 pounds crabmeat	¼ cup flour
1 bunch green onions, diced	Salt and finely ground black pepper to taste
5 raw eggs	4 tablespoons Old Bay Seasoning
½ cup Italian bread crumbs	Olive oil

Mix all of the above together and form 24 (4-ounce) cakes. Sauté 3 cakes at a time in 4 ounces of olive oil. Cook each side for approximately 4 minutes.

PINEAPPLE SALSA:

5 cups diced pineapple	1 bunch cilantro, finely diced
1 red bell pepper, diced	1 lime, juiced
1 gold bell pepper, diced	Salt and pepper to taste
1 green bell pepper, diced	
1 cup diced yellow onion	

Mix all ingredients together and chill for at least 2 hours.

Place 4 ounces Pineapple Salsa in center of plate surrounded by 3 crab cakes. Garnish with chopped parsley and lemon wedges.

Callaway Gardens

P. O. Box 2000
Pine Mountain, GA 31822-2000
1-800-Callaway (225-5292)
www.callawayonline.com

Rachel M. Crumbley
Manager of Corporate Relations

Thierry Connault
Executive Chef

Callaway is a man-made landscape in a unique natural setting, which was conceived and created by Cason J. Callaway and his wife, Virginia Hand Callaway, for the benefit of mankind. The purpose is to provide a wholesome family environment where all may find beauty, relaxation, inspiration, and a better understanding of the living world. Callaway, a public, educational, horticultural, and charitable organization, is owned and operated by the nonprofit Ida Cason Callaway Foundation. Its wholly owned subsidiary, Callaway Gardens Resort, Inc., a regular business corporation, operates the recreational, lodging, and retail facilities at Callaway. After-tax proceeds go to the foundation to support its efforts.

Pecan Crusted Chicken, Muscadine Syrup, Orange and Ginger Sauce

MUSCADINE SYRUP:

½ cup white vinegar	½ cup vegetable oil
½ cup red wine vinegar	1 cup muscadine
1 teaspoon salt	preserves
½ teaspoon white pepper	

In a food processor on medium speed, blend white and red vinegar with salt and pepper. Add oil. Add muscadine preserves and mix well to achieve a creamy consistency. Store in your refrigerator up to one month. Voilà, you can recreate some of the Callaway magic in your home!

2 cups flour	Peanut oil
Salt and pepper	Butter
3 eggs	½ cup Muscadine Syrup
6 ounces pecan meal	2 cups orange juice
4 ounces bread crumbs	2 teaspoons ginger powder
8 (6- to 8-ounce) skinless,	3 cups heavy cream
boneless chicken	Juice of one lemon
breasts	

Combine in three separate deep dishes: flour seasoned with salt and pepper; beaten eggs; and pecan meal mix with bread crumbs. Place in that order.

Pat chicken dry, roll in flour, and lightly shake off excess. Then dredge chicken pieces in eggs, again shake off excess and roll in pecan and bread crumb mix. Cook chicken in a skillet over medium heat with a combination of peanut oil and butter. Be careful not to burn the crust.

In a saucepan over medium heat, bring Muscadine Syrup to a boil. Add orange juice and ginger powder. Let it reduce by ¾ and add cream. Reduce again by ¼ in order to obtain a creamy consistency. Add a touch of lemon juice to counteract the sweetness of the sauce. Make sure you taste during the process to reach the taste you prefer. Serve with vegetable (sautéed spinach goes great with it!). Serves 8.

Callaway Short Bread with Georgia Peaches Flambé

⅓ cup granulated sugar	1¼ cups heavy cream
2 cups all-purpose flour	8 fresh peaches
2½ teaspoons baking	1 cup honey
powder	¼ cup Jack Daniel's
½ teaspoon salt	bourbon
6 tablespoons butter	

In a bowl, combine sugar, flour, baking powder, and salt. Cut butter into small pieces and add. Make sure butter is incorporated, then add cream. Do not over-work the dough. The process should take less than 2 minutes.

Let the dough rest for 10 to 15 minutes with a cloth on top to prevent drying. On a floury surface, lay dough at about ½-inch thickness and use a cutter to cut the dough. Cook on a greased pan at 350° for 10 to 15 minutes.

Peel and cut into wedges the fresh peaches. Pour honey in a pan and bring to a boil; pour peaches in it. Stir for about 3 to 4 minutes and flambé with Jack Daniel's. To serve, place shortbread on a dish and scoop peaches on top. Serves 8.

Stone Creek Golf & Country Club

4300 Coleman Road
Valdosta, GA 31602
(229) 293-2527

Chef Kimberly A. Watson

Peppered Cottage Cheese Dip

1 (1-pound) tub small curd
cottage cheese
1 tablespoon course-
ground pepper

$\frac{1}{4}$ teaspoon fresh-minced
garlic
Pinch salt

In a glass bowl, hand-mix all ingredients. Cover and chill at least one hour, overnight is best for flavor to set in. Serves as a dip for fresh vegetables, and is even great with potato chips. Serves 4 to 6.

French Vanilla Cream Pie

1 (8- or 9-inch) graham
cracker crust
1$\frac{1}{4}$ cups milk

1$\frac{1}{4}$ cups sour cream
1 (3-ounce) package
French vanilla pudding

If using homemade, bake graham cracker crust and set aside to cool. With a hand mixer, beat together milk and sour cream until smooth. Blend in dry pudding mix until slightly thickened. Pour into crust. Chill 1 to 2 hours. Serve with fresh fruit or whipped topping.

Fiesta Eggs Benedict

8 large eggs
6 English muffins, split in
halves
12 breakfast sausage patties

$\frac{1}{2}$ cup milk
1 (10$\frac{3}{4}$-ounce) can nacho
cheese soup

Scramble eggs in nonstick pan so no oil is needed; set aside. Toast or flat grill English muffins. Do not butter. Fry or broil breakfast sausage. Pat dry on paper towel to remove grease. In a small saucepan, blend and heat milk and nacho cheese soup. Build your creation starting with $\frac{1}{2}$ muffin, sausage patty, and scoop of scrambled eggs, then smother with nacho cheese soup. Great in the morning or evening with grits, hash browns, fruit, or even steamed vegetables. Serves 6 to 12.

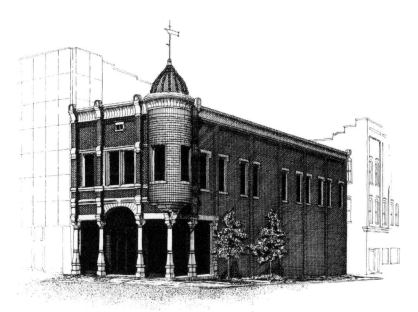

C. C. Varnedoe & Company, Valdosta

Special Section

Special Section Menu

Bailey Family Recipes

8755 Monte Carlo Cove
Germantown, TN 38139

Ann Freeman Bailey, Executive Chef
John M. Bailey, Author and Sous Chef

Red Beans and Rice

1 pound dry red beans	$2/3$ cup chopped green pepper
2 quarts water	
3 tablespoons vegetable oil	1 bay leaf
2 pounds smoked sausage, cut in 1-inch pieces	1 teaspoon Worcestershire sauce
3 cloves garlic, pressed	$1/2$ teaspoon Tabasco sauce
$1^1/2$ cups chopped yellow onions	
$3/4$ cup chopped green onions	1 tablespoon minced fresh parsley
$1^1/2$ cups chopped celery	$1^1/2$ teaspoons salt
	3 cups steamed rice

Rinse and drain beans. In a large pot with a lid, place beans and cover with water. Add vegetable oil and bring to a boil. Reduce heat and simmer 40 minutes.

Add sausage, cover, and cook 1 hour, stirring occasionally. Add garlic, onions, celery, green pepper, and bay leaf. Continue cooking, covered $1^1/2$ hours or until soft. Add Worcestershire, Tabasco sauce, parsley, and salt. Simmer 5 minutes. Remove bay leaf and serve over rice. Serves 6.

Potato Casserole

6 to 8 large potatoes
1 stick butter
2 cups grated Kraft Old
  English cheese
1/4 cup whole milk

1 bunch green onions
  (tops and bottoms),
  chopped
2 cups sour cream
Salt to taste

Boil potatoes in jackets in salted water; chill. Peel when cold and grate potatoes. Melt butter and cheese in skillet with milk. Add onions and sour cream. Mix in potatoes. Season to taste. Put in large buttered casserole dish. If possible, chill several hours or overnight. Bake at 350° for about 45 minutes or until hot. Serves 6.

Crab Imperial

1/2 cup margarine
1 teaspoon grated onion
1/2 cup flour
2 cups scalded cream
3 egg yolks
2 tablespoons finely
  chopped parsley
Salt and pepper to taste
1 teaspoon minced chives
2 tablespoons finely
  chopped mushrooms
1 tablespoon
  Worcestershire sauce

3 tablespoons sherry
1 teaspoon prepared
  mustard
1 pound crabmeat in
  lumps, carefully picked
  over
1 hard-boiled egg,
  chopped
Bread crumbs
3 tablespoons grated
  Swiss cheese

Melt margarine; add grated onion and flour. Stir (do not brown) and gradually add cream. Continue stirring until thick and smooth. Mix in egg yolks, one at a time. Stirring briskly, with last yolk, add parsley, salt, pepper, chives, mushrooms, Worcestershire sauce, sherry, and mustard. Heat well (do not boil) and add crabmeat and hard-boiled egg. Fill 6 to 8 shells or ramekins. Sprinkle bread crumbs and grated cheese on top. Broil until bubbly and light brown. Serves 6 to 8.

Seafood Gumbo

1/2 cup vegetable oil
1/2 cup all-purpose flour
1 1/2 cups chopped onions
1 (8-ounce) can tomato
  sauce
6 cups hot water
3/4 cup chopped green
  pepper
2 large garlic cloves,
  pressed

1 tablespoon salt
3/4 teaspoon cayenne
  pepper
2 pounds shrimp, peeled
  and deveined
1/4 cup chopped green
  onion tops
1/4 cup chopped fresh
  parsley
3 cups steamed rice

In a Dutch oven, heat oil and gradually add flour, stirring constantly over medium-low heat until roux is dark brown, about 40 minutes (do not burn). Add onions and cook until tender. Add tomato sauce and cook over low heat for 15 minutes. Slowly add water, stirring until smooth. Add green pepper, garlic, salt, and cayenne; bring to a boil. Reduce heat and simmer 40 minutes. Add shrimp and onion tops; simmer for 15 minutes. Add parsley and serve over rice. Serves 6.

Italian Spinach

3 (10-ounce) boxes frozen
  leaf spinach
Salt to taste
1/4 cup olive oil
2 or 3 cloves fresh garlic,
  minced

3 eggs, beaten
Parmesan cheese
2 slices mozzarella
  cheese

Cook spinach (salt to taste) and drain very well (press water out with paper towels). Heat olive oil in skillet with garlic (don't burn the garlic). Add spinach and beaten eggs to oil. Stir (over low heat) until the eggs are cooked. Add Parmesan and mozzarella cheese to spinach. Stir until cheese melts. Ready to serve. Great as side dish with pasta or steak. Serves 4.

Italian Tomato Sauce

6 to 8 links sweet Italian
  sausage
12 to 16 small meatballs
2 (28-ounce) cans tomato
  purée
2 (28-ounce) cans crushed
  tomatoes, strained
1 teaspoon garlic salt
1 teaspoon crushed basil
1 tablespoon sugar
Pasta

Bake sausage and meatballs for 20 minutes on each side in a 350° oven. Combine tomato purée and tomatoes in a 4-quart pot; add seasoning, sugar, sausage, and meatballs. Simmer for about 2 hours, stirring occasionally. Add water if sauce becomes too thick. Serve over pasta. Serves 8. Freezes well.

Lasagna

$\frac{1}{4}$ cup chopped celery
1 medium onion, chopped
1 clove garlic, minced
2 tablespoons olive oil
1 to 2 pounds ground beef
2 (14$\frac{1}{2}$-ounce) cans
  tomatoes
1 (6-ounce) can tomato
  paste
2 teaspoons salt
$\frac{1}{4}$ teaspoon cayenne
  pepper
$\frac{1}{2}$ teaspoon oregano
1 bay leaf
1 (8-ounce) package
  lasagna or broad
  egg noodles
2 cups ricotta or cottage
  cheese
1 pound mozzarella
  cheese, sliced
$\frac{1}{3}$ cup grated Parmesan
  cheese

Cook celery, onion, and garlic in olive oil until tender. Add ground beef and brown until crumbly but not hard. Drain. Add tomatoes, tomato paste, salt, cayenne pepper, oregano, and bay leaf. Cook noodles in boiling water until tender. Drain. Arrange half of noodles and cover with a layer of ricotta and mozzarella cheese. Repeat with remaining noodles, meat sauce, and mozzarella. Sprinkle with Parmesan cheese. Bake in a 350° oven for 30 minutes. Serves 8 to 10.

Fettuccine Alfredo

10 to 12 ounces fettuccine
  (or other wide noodles)
2 tablespoons butter

Cook noodles according to package directions. Drain and toss lightly with 2 tablespoons butter. Keep hot.

SAUCE:
1$\frac{1}{2}$ sticks margarine
1 cup half-and-half
1$\frac{1}{2}$ cups freshly grated
  Parmesan cheese
3 tablespoons minced
  onion
3 to 4 tablespoons minced
  chives
2 tablespoons fresh
  chopped parsley
1 cup sour cream
Dash of garlic salt
Hot noodles

Melt butter on low heat and add half-and-half. Blend in cheese and stir until melted. Add remaining ingredients and stir over low heat; do not boil. Add this sauce to hot noodles and toss well to blend. Serves 4 to 6.

Chicken Parmesan

2 cups seasoned bread
  crumbs
$\frac{1}{2}$ cup grated Parmesan
  cheese
$\frac{1}{3}$ cup chopped parsley
1 (2.8-ounce) can onion
  rings, crushed
1 stick margarine
2 garlic cloves, crushed
1 teaspoon
  Worcestershire sauce
1 teaspoon dry mustard
4 whole chicken breasts,
  boned, skinned, and
  split

Combine first 4 ingredients, mixing well. Melt margarine in saucepan and sauté garlic. Stir in Worcestershire sauce and mustard. Dip chicken in margarine mixture and then in bread crumb mixture. Coat well. Place in large foil-lined baking dish. Pour remaining margarine mixture over all. Bake in 350° oven for 40 to 45 minutes. Serves 8.

Chicken Pot Pie

2½ to 3 pounds chicken breasts or whole chicken
2 stalks celery, chopped
1 small onion, chopped
1 bay leaf
½ lemon
Salt and pepper to taste
Poultry seasoning to taste
2 cups reserved broth

1 (10¾-ounce) can cream of chicken soup
2 hard-boiled eggs, chopped
1 (10-ounce) package early June peas, cooked and drained
Several carrots, chopped, cooked, and drained

Cook chicken and next 6 ingredients with enough water to cover. Cool and save 2 cups broth. Remove meat from bones and cut up. Place in an 8x11-inch greased casserole dish. Combine reserved broth with soup and heat. Add eggs, peas, and carrots to broth, then pour over chicken.

CRUST:

1 stick margarine, melted
½ teaspoon black pepper
1 teaspoon salt

1 cup self-rising flour
1 cup buttermilk
Poultry seasoning to taste

Mix ingredients together. Spread on top of casserole with spoon. Bake at 350° for 25 to 30 minutes or until bubbly and crust is light brown. Serves 4 to 6.

Deep-Fried Chicken

1 chicken fryer, skin removed, cut up
1 cup buttermilk
1½ to 2 teaspoons salt

½ teaspoon black pepper
1 cup flour
1 teaspoon paprika
4 to 6 cups shortening

Place chicken pieces into a bowl and pour buttermilk over. Let rest for 30 minutes in refrigerator, turning occasionally.

Mix dry ingredients and place in a paper bag. Drain chicken pieces and add to bag. Shake vigorously until all pieces have been coated. Place chicken pieces on a plate and refrigerate for 30 minutes. Heat shortening in a deep skillet or fryer, deep enough to cover chicken. When shortening has reached 375° or sizzles when a drop of bread is added, add thighs and drumsticks and cook for about 7 minutes. Then add white meat and cook for another 8 minutes or until all pieces are golden brown and tender.

Quail

8 fresh quail, cleaned
1 stick margarine
Juice of 1 lemon
1 small onion, sliced
½ lemon, sliced

¼ cup Worcestershire sauce
Salt and pepper to taste
1½ cups chicken broth
½ cup white wine

Brown quail in margarine in an iron skillet. In a saucepan, heat lemon juice, onion, lemon slices, Worcestershire sauce, salt and pepper. Simmer 5 minutes. Remove onion and lemon slices and pour liquid over quail. Cook uncovered for 1 hour over low heat. During the last half-hour, add white wine.

Beef Tenderloin

1 heaping teaspoon thyme
1 teaspoon black pepper
1 teaspoon garlic salt
1 tablespoon salt

¼ teaspoon oregano
1 beef tenderloin
1½ cups water

Mix spices and rub on tenderloin (most are the same size and will serve about 10 people). Wrap meat in foil and refrigerate overnight, or freeze. Take meat out of refrigerator 2 hours before cooking and allow to come to room temperature. If frozen, allow meat to thaw completely.

Preheat oven to 400°. Remove meat from foil and place in pan with water. Cook about 25 minutes for rare meat. Check every 5 minutes thereafter if you prefer your meat more well-done.

Crab Mornay

½ cup margarine
1 onion, peeled and chopped
2 celery stalks, trimmed and chopped
1 garlic clove, peeled and crushed
½ teaspoon dried parsley
¼ cup self-rising flour
1½ cups light cream
1½ cups chicken broth

1 cup grated Gruyère or Swiss cheese
½ teaspoon grated lemon rind
1 pound white crabmeat, drained and flaked
1 teaspoon lemon juice
2 tablespoons sherry
Milk
Paprika

In a medium to large skillet, melt margarine over medium heat and cook onion, celery, and garlic for 2 to 3 minutes. Add parsley and flour and stir well to make a roux or paste. Add cream and broth and stir with a whisk. Let heat until starting to thicken. When thick, lower heat and add cheese. Whisk until cheese is melted. (Sauce can be made at this point up to 2 days in advance.)

While sauce is hot or reheated and smooth, add lemon zest, crabmeat, lemon juice, and sherry. Add milk, as needed for desired consistency, by teaspoonfuls. This should be served in individual greased shells or a greased 1-quart oven-proof casserole. Sprinkle top with paprika. Dish can be refrigerated, covered, for up to 24 hours at this point.

Bake at 350° for 10 to 25 minutes depending on size of dish. Should be bubbly around edges. Serves 4 to 6.

Baked Snapper or Grouper

3 snapper or grouper fillets, fresh or frozen
2 tomatoes
6 green onions
1 cup fresh mushrooms

1 green bell pepper
1 teaspoon lemon pepper
1 teaspoon garlic salt
1 cup Italian dressing
Lemon wedges

Place fish on foil in baking dish. Chop vegetables and sprinkle on fish along with lemon pepper and garlic salt. Pour Italian dressing over top. Cover with foil and bake in 350° oven for 30 minutes. Garnish with lemon wedges. Serve with yellow rice. Serves 3 to 4.

Creole Shrimp

¼ cup chopped onion
½ bell pepper, chopped
2 tablespoons vegetable oil
2 cups stewed tomatoes
¼ cup chili sauce
Salt, pepper, and Worcestershire sauce to taste

1 pound boiled shrimp, shelled and deveined
1 cup rice, cooked

Sauté onions and bell pepper in vegetable oil. Drain off some of the oil. Add tomatoes, chili sauce, and seasonings. Cook until thick, then add shrimp just long enough to heat through. Serve hot over rice. Serves 4.

Shrimp Scampi

GARLIC BUTTER SAUCE:
½ cup margarine or butter

4 garlic cloves, pressed
¼ teaspoon minced chives

Combine all ingredients and cook 1 minute.

2 tablespoons grated Parmesan cheese
1 pound shrimp, shelled and deveined, cooked with 1 teaspoon vinegar added to water for 3 minutes

4 slices lemon, cut up, for garnish

Combine Garlic Butter Sauce and Parmesan cheese in a saucepan. Heat until cheese melts. Place shrimp in baking dish and pour sauce over. Bake in 300° oven for 5 minutes. Garnish with lemon slices. Serves 12.

Oyster Stew

1 quart oysters, drained
4 cups light cream
2 cups milk
¼ cup margarine
½ teaspoon salt

Dash of pepper
½ teaspoon
  Worcestershire sauce
Paprika

Combine all ingredients except paprika in heavy saucepan. Bring to a low boil. Cook until edges of oysters begin to curl. Remove from heat and serve immediately with a dash of paprika. Serves 6.

Coconut Pound Cake

3 sticks butter, softened
3 cups sugar
6 eggs
3 cups all-purpose flour
¼ teaspoon baking soda

¼ teaspoon salt
1 cup sour cream
1 teaspoon vanilla
1 (6-ounce) package
  frozen coconut, thawed

Prepare a tube pan by rubbing with vegetable shortening. Add flour and shake to cover. Place butter in bowl and cream well. Add sugar slowly as you mix. Add eggs, one at a time, and beat. Sift flour with soda and salt. Alternate adding flour mixture and sour cream in thirds until well mixed. Add vanilla. Fold in coconut. Pour into prepared pan and bake at 350° for approximately 1 hour and 15 minutes to 1 hour and 30 minutes. Yields 1 cake.

Key Lime Pie

1 (14-ounce) can
  sweetened condensed
  milk
1 (6-ounce) can frozen
  limeade, slightly thawed
1 (8-ounce) container Cool
  Whip topping

Few drops of green
  food coloring (optional)
1 graham cracker pie
  crust

Combine condensed milk, limeade, and Cool Whip. Fold mixture until blended. Pour into graham cracker crust. Chill. Garnish, if desired, with extra whipped cream and lime slices.

Glossary

aïoli ~ A garlic mayonnaise from France usually served with seafood.

al dente ~ An Italian phrase used to describe pasta or vegetables cooked just until firm, not soft or overdone.

ancho ~ A fairly mild red chile pepper.

andouille ~ A thick Acadian sausage of lean smoked pork, ranging from bland to very peppery.

anise ~ An herb that tastes like licorice. It is often used in pastries, cheeses, etc.

antipasto ~ An appetizer that is generally served before pasta.

appareil ~ A mixture of ingredients already prepared for use in a recipe.

Arborio rice ~ An Italian medium-grain rice that is used frequently for risotto.

arugula ~ A leafy salad herb that has an aromatic peppery flavor.

baguette ~ A French bread that's been formed into a long, narrow cylindrical loaf.

bain-marie ~ (Water bath) consists of a bowl placed over a bowl of boiling hot water to gently cook the sauce, etc., without overcooking.

balsamic vinegar ~ A very fine, aged vinegar made in Modena, Italy, from white Trebbiano grape juice.

basil ~ An aromatic herb widely used in Mediterranean cooking. It is used in pesto sauce, salads, and cooking fish.

basmati rice ~ A long-grain rice with a nutty flavor.

bay leaf ~ This aromatic herb comes from the evergreen bay laurel tree, native to the Mediterranean. Dried bay leaves are used frequently in poultry, fish, and meat dishes as well as stocks and soups.

béarnaise ~ One of the classic French sauces. It is made with emulsified egg yolks, butter, fresh herbs, and shallots. It is often served with meat, grilled fish and vegetables.

béchamel ~ One of the basic French sauces. It is a sauce made from white roux, milk or cream, onions, and seasonings.

beignet ~ A French word for batter-dipped, fried fritters, usually sweet like a doughnut, and dusted with confectioners' sugar.

beurre blanc ~ A white butter sauce made from shallots, white wine vinegar, and white wine that has been reduced and thickened with heavy cream and unsalted butter.

beurre manié ~ A paste of flour and butter used to thicken sauces.

bisque ~ A thick, rich soup usually made from puréed seafood (oysters, shrimp, or lobster) and thickened with cream.

blanch ~ To plunge fruits and vegetables into boiling water briefly, then into cold water to stop the cooking process.

bon appétit ~ Literally, "good appetite" or "enjoy your meal."

boudin blanc ~ A peppery, pale-brown link of pork meat, liver, onions, and other seasonings. Rice is usually what binds the fillings of this richly seasoned sausage.

braise ~ The slow cooking of food in a tightly covered container with a flavoring liquid equal to about half the amount of the main ingredient.

Brie ~ A soft cows' milk cheese made in the French region of Brie.

brûlée ~ A French word for "burnt" and refers to a caramelized coating of sugar, such as a topping for crème brûlée.

brunoise ~ Vegetables that have been finely diced or shredded, then cooked slowly in butter.

bruschetta ~ Toasted bread slices rubbed with garlic and drizzled with extra virgin olive oil.

café au lait ~ Coffee and chicory blend with milk; usually a half-and-half mixture of hot coffee and hot milk.

Cajun ~ Slang for Acadians, the French-speaking people who migrated to south Louisiana from Nova Scotia in the 18th century. Cajuns were happily removed from city life, preferring a rustic life along the bayous. The term now applies to the people, the culture, and the cooking.

cannelloni ~ Large, round tubes, typically stuffed then baked with a sauce.

caper ~ The pickled bud of a flowering caper plant. It is found on the Mediterranean coast. Capers are often used as a condiment in salads, in making tartar sauce, and as a seasoning in broiling fish.

capon ~ A castrated young male chicken, fed a fattening diet and brought to market before it is ten months old.

caramel ~ Sugar that has been cooked until it melts and becomes a golden brown color.

cardamom ~ A member of the ginger family. It has a spicy flavor and is used in Indian and Middle Eastern dishes.

caul fat ~ Considered superior, this thin fatty membrane which lines the abdominal cavity is usually taken from pigs or sheet, and resembles a lacy net.

cayenne pepper ~ Red chile pepper that is dried and ground fine for home use.

chaurice ~ A highly spiced pork or beef sausage used in Cajun cooking.

chervil ~ An herb belonging to the parsley family. It is best used fresh because of its delicate flavor.

chicory ~ An herb, the roots of which are dried, ground, and roasted and used to flavor coffee.

chiffonade ~ Leafy vegetables such as spinach and lettuce cut into thin strips.

Chinese five-spice powder ~ Used extensively in Chinese cooking, this pungent mixture of 5 ground spices usually consists of equal parts of cinnamon, cloves, fennel seed, star anise, and Szechuan peppercorns.

chipotle ~ A brownish-red chile pepper that has been dried and smoked and sometimes canned. This chile pepper has a smoky flavor and is very hot.

chives ~ A member of the onion family used in flavoring foods.

chutney ~ A sweet and/or sour seasoning that can be made from fruits and vegetables and flavored with many kinds of spices.

ciabatta ~ Italian bread named for its slipper shape.

cilantro ~ A fresh coriander leaf.

clarified butter ~ Butter that has been heated to remove the impurities.

clarify ~ To remove all impurities.

concassé ~ Any mixture that has been ground or coarsely chopped, such as a tomato concassé

condiment ~ Any seasoning, spice, sauce, relish, etc., used to enhance food at the table.

consommé ~ A clear strained stock, usually clarified, made from poultry, fish, meat, or game and flavored with vegetables.

coriander ~ A member of the carrot family. Fresh coriander is also called cilantro. This herb is prized for its dried seeds and fresh leaves and is used in similar ways to parsley.

coulis ~ A thick sauce or purée made from cooked vegetables, fruits, etc.

court-bouillon ~ A rich, spicy soup, or stew, made with fish fillet, tomatoes, onions, and sometimes mixed vegetables.

couscous ~ Traditional couscous is generally made from coarsely ground semolina, a wheat flour used for pasta. It is popular in the Mediterranean areas of Morocco and Algeria. It is often served over vegetables or meats along with sauces.

crème brûlée ~ A custard made from eggs and covered with a "burnt" layer of sugar which has caramelized in the oven.

crème fraîche ~ Made from un-pasteurized cream with an additive such as yogurt which gives it a distinctive flavor.

Creole ~ The word originally described those people of mixed French and Spanish blood who migrated from Europe or were born in southeast Louisiana.

The term has expanded and now embraces a type of cuisine and a style of architecture.

crevette ~ The French word for "shrimp."

cumin ~ A spice from the seeds of the cumin plant. It is often used in making pickles, chutneys, and especially curries.

currant ~ A fruit used to make jams and jellies. It is also used as a glaze for meats. The red variety is widely used.

curry powder ~ A mixture of spices widely used in preparing and cooking meats and vegetables. It is often used in Indian cooking.

daikon ~ A large radish.

deglaze ~ A process of dissolving cooking juices left in a pan where meats or poultry have been cooked. This is achieved by adding liquids such as stock or wines to the sediment and then reducing it to half the volume. The sauce is the strained and seasoned.

demi-glace ~ A brown sauce boiled and reduced by half.

Dijon mustard ~ Mustard made from a white wine base.

dill ~ An herb used with vinegar to pickle cucumbers. It is also used to flavor foods.

dirty rice ~ Pan-fried, leftover cooked rice sautéed with green peppers, onions, celery, stock, liver, giblets, and many other ingredients.

dredge ~ To coat food with a dry ingredient such as bread crumbs, cornmeal, or flour.

Dungeness crab ~ A large rock crab found in the Pacific Northwest.

espagnole sauce ~ A rich, reduced brown stock containing herbs, tomato purée, or fresh tomatoes and a mixture of browned vegetables, all thickened by brown roux.

étouffée ~ A succulent Cajun dish made from a spicy roux and crawfish or shrimp along with vegetables (usually celery, bell peppers, and onions) which is served over rice.

fagioli ~ The Italian word for "beans."

fais do-do ~ The name for a lively party where traditional Cajun dance is performed.

farfalle ~ Butterfly-shaped pasta.

fennel ~ A vegetable bulb or herb with a spicy flavor. It is often used in soups and salads.

feta cheese ~ A soft and crumbly goat's milk cheese often used in salads and Greek dishes.

filé powder ~ Sassafras leaves that have been dried and used in the final stages to thicken and flavor gumbo. Okra can also be used to thicken gumbo instead of filé powder.

filo; phyllo ~ A very thin dough that contains little fat and is used for strudel, baklava, and other pastries.

flan ~ An open custard tart made in a mold. Caramel cream custard is a popular flan dessert.

foie gras ~ The enlarged liver of a fattened or force-fed goose.

frais, fraîche ~ Fresh.

fraise ~ French for "strawberry."

free-range ~ Poultry or animals allowed to roam and feed without confinement, as opposed to commercially bred animals, which are caged.

fumet ~ Liquid that gives flavor and body to sauces and stocks. Fish fumet is used to poach fish fillets. It is made from dry white wine, fish stock, and bouquet garni.

garde manger ~ Pantry area where a cold buffet can be prepared.

garnish ~ A small amount of a flavorful, edible ingredient added as trimmings to complement the main dish and enhance its appearance.

ginger ~ A spice from a rhizome of a plant native to China. It is used fresh in Chinese cooking, but can also be used dried or ground.

glace ~ Ice cream; also used for cake icing.

glaze ~ It is used as a coating to give a shiny appearance to roasts, poultry, custards, jams, and jellies.

lutinous rice ~ Sticky rice used by the Japanese to make sushi and rice cakes.

Gorgonzola ~ A strong Italian blue cheese.

gratons ~ The Acadian-French word for fatty pork skins fried in lard (also known as cracklings).

grillades ~ Squares of braised beef or veal. Grillades and grits is a popular local breakfast.

guava ~ A sweet, fragrant tropical fruit. It makes delicious jellies.

gumbo ~ A Cajun or Creole soup thickened with okra or filé powder. Gumbo is an African word for "okra."

habanero ~ An extremely hot chile pepper, oval-shaped and smaller than the jalapeño. The color changes from green to orange and red upon ripening. It is used in stews and sauces.

haddock ~ Closely related to a cod but smaller and thin-skinned. It is excellent broiled in butter.

halibut ~ The largest member of the flounder family. It can be smoked, broiled, or grilled.

haricot vert ~ French for "green string beans."

herbs de Provence ~ A mixture of assorted dried herbs which commonly contains basil, fennel seed, lavender, marjoram, rosemary, sage, summer savory, and thyme.

Herbsaint ~ Anise liqueur-tastes like licorice.

hoisin sauce ~ A thick brown sauce made from soybeans, garlic, sugar, and salt which is used in Chinese cooking to flavor sauces and marinades.

hollandaise ~ One of the classic sauces in French cooking. It is made from an emulsion of hot clarified butter and eggs lightly heated until it begins to have the consistency of a smooth custard. It also contains lemons and shallots.

infuse ~ To soak spices, herbs, or vegetables in a liquid to extract their flavor.

jalapeño ~ A very hot green chile pepper generally used fresh, but also available canned.

jambalaya ~ A Cajun dish of rice, shrimp, crawfish, sausage, chicken, and beans, seasoned with Creole spices.

julienne ~ Vegetables cut into thin strips.

kalamata olive ~ Large, black Greek olive.

kale ~ A frilly, leafy vegetable of the cabbage family.

King Cake ~ A ring-shaped pastry decorated with colored sugar in the traditional Mardi Gras colors, purple, green, and gold, that represent justice, faith, and power. A small plastic baby is hidden inside the cake and the person who finds it must provide the next King Cake.

lagniappe ~ This word is Cajun for "something extra," like the extra doughnut in a baker's dozen. An unexpected nice surprise.

leek ~ A member of the onion family that is used in soups, casseroles, etc.

loganberry ~ Similar to a blackberry and raspberry, it can be served with cream as a dessert, a filling for tarts, or as a cream pudding.

mandoline ~ A tool use to cut vegetables evenly into thick or thin slices.

mango ~ A delicious, sweet tropical fruit often served alone as a dessert or used in cooking preserves and chutneys.

marinade ~ A liquid, including seasonings, to flavor and tenderize fish, meat, and poultry before cooking.

marinara ~ A tomato sauce flavored with herbs and garlic, usually served with pasta.

Merlot ~ A red-wine grape that produces a fruity flavor.

mesclun ~ A mixture of wild salad leaves and herbs. They are generally served with dressing containing walnut or olive oil and wine vinegar.

mirepoix ~ A mixture of cut vegetables—usually carrot, onion, celery, and sometimes ham or bacon—used to flavor sauces and as a bed on which to braise meat.

mirin ~ A sweet and syrupy Japanese rice wine used for cooking.

mirliton ~ A hard-shelled squash.

miso ~ A soybean paste.

Mornay Sauce ~ A classic French sauce; béchamel sauce to which egg yolks, cream, and cheese are added.

muffuletta ~ This huge sandwich is made up of thick layers of several different types of Italian meats and cheeses and a layer of olive salad. Served on special Muffuletta bread.

oregano ~ Oregano is an herb very similar to marjoram but more pungent. It is widely used in Greek and Italian cooking.

orzo ~ Rice-shaped pasta.

panache ~ French to describe something mixed or multicolored such as salads, fruit, or ice cream.

panéed ~ Breaded and pan-fried.

pancetta ~ Italian bacon that is sometimes rolled into a solid round.

paprika ~ A variety of red bell pepper that has been dried and powdered and made into a cooking spice. It is used in making Hungarian goulash, etc.

penne ~ Tube-shaped pasta cut on the diagonal.

peperonata ~ An Italian dish of bell peppers, tomatoes, onions, and garlic cooked in olive oil. It can be served hot or cold.

pepperoncini; peperoncini ~ A hot red chile pepper served fresh or dried.

pepperoni ~ An Italian salami of pork and beef seasoned with hot red peppers.

phyllo ~ See filo.

picante sauce; piccante sauce ~ Hot spicy tomato-based sauce.

piccata ~ Veal scallop.

plantain ~ A tropical fruit similar to the banana.

po-boy ~ A type of sandwich which started out as an inexpensive meal. There are fried oyster po-boys, shrimp po-boys, and others. All are served on French bread.

poisson ~ French for "fish."

poivre ~ French for "pepper."

omodoro ~ Italian for "tomato."

orcini ~ Italian for "wild mushrooms."

portobello mushroom ~ A large cultivated field mushroom which has a firm texture and is ideal for grilling and as a meat substitute.

praline ~ A sweet candy patty. The main ingredients are sugar, water and pecans.

prawn ~ A large shrimp.

prosciutto ~ Italian ham cured by salting and air drying.

purée ~ Food that is pounded, finely chopped, or processed through a blender or strained through a sieve to achieve a smooth consistency.

quiche ~ A custard-filled tart with a savory flavor.

radicchio ~ A reddish member of the chicory family used as a garnish or for salad.

ratatouille ~ A mixture of tomatoes, eggplants, zucchini, bell peppers, and onions cooked in olive oil. It can be served hot or cold.

red beans and rice ~ Red beans cooked in seasonings and spices and usually with chunks of sausage and ham—served over a bed of rice.

reduce ~ To boil down a liquid to thicken its consistency and concentrate its flavor.

relleno ~ Stuffing.

rémoulade ~ One of the classic French sauces. It is made from mayonnaise seasoned with chopped eggs and gherkins, parsley, capers, tarragon, and shallots. It is served with shellfish, vegetables, and cold meats.

rice wine ~ Distilled from fermented rice.

ricotta ~ The word ricotta means "recooked" in Italian. It is a soft cheese made from whey and has a slight sweet taste.

rigatoni ~ Italian macaroni.

riso ~ Italian for "rice." A rice-shaped pasta; used to make risotto, an Italian rice dish.

risotto ~ An Italian arborio rice dish simmered slowly.

roghan josh ~ A spicy lamb dish from India, red in color and served with rice.

rosemary ~ A shrub with aromatic needle-like leaves. It is used fresh or dried as an herb, especially with lamb, pork, and veal.

rouille ~ A spicy red pepper and garlic mayonnaise.

roulade ~ French for a rolled slice of meat or piece of fish filled with a savory stuffing.

roux ~ A mixture of flour and fat (usually butter or shortening) cooked together slowly to form a thickening agent for sauces, gumbos, and other soups.

sec ~ French for "dry."

scaloppine, scaloppina ~ An Italian term for a thin scallop of meat. The meat is dredged in flour, then sautéed and served variously.

shallot ~ A sweet member of the onion family. It has a more delicate flavor than regular onions. It is used extensively in French cooking.

shiitake ~ A dark brown mushroom with a meaty flavor. It is available both fresh and dried. It was originally from Japan but is now cultivated in both America and Europe.

slurry ~ A thin paste of water and flour (or cornstarch), which is stirred into hot preparations (such as soups, stews, and sauces) as a thickener. After the slurry is added, the mixture should be stirred and cooked for several minutes in order for the flour to lose its raw taste.

sommelier ~ Wine steward.

sorrel ~ A leafy plant often used in salads, soups, omelets, purées, and sauces. It has a distinct lemon taste.

sweat ~ To cook in a little fat (in a covered pot) over very low heat, so that the food exudes some of its juice without browning: used especially with vegetables.

tamari ~ Similar to but thicker than soy sauce, tamari is also a dark sauce made from soybeans.

tapenade ~ A thick paste made from capers, anchovies, ripe olives, olive oil, lemon juice, seasonings, and sometimes small pieces of tuna.

tartar ~ A sauce made with mayonnaise, egg yolks, chopped onions, capers, and chives. It is often served with fish, meat, and poultry.

tasso ~ A highly seasoned Cajun sausage made from pork.

thyme ~ An herb with a pungent smell that belongs to the same family as mint. It is used in soups, stocks, casseroles, and stews.

timbale ~ Metal mold shaped like a drum.

tofu ~ A white Japanese bean curd made from minced soy beans boiled in water then strained and coagulated with sea water. It is soft and easily digested.

tomatillo ~ Mexican fruit related to the tomato. It is often used in salsa, salads, sauces, etc.

tournedo ~ A trimmed cut of beef or veal fillet.

U10 or U12 jumbo shrimp ~ 10 or 12 shrimp to a pound.

veal ~ The meat of milk-fed baby calves.

vermicelli ~ A thin Italian pasta.

vinaigrette ~ A basic dressing of oil and vinegar with salt, pepper, herbs, and sometimes mustard.

white sauce ~ Béchamel or velouté sauce, both made from roux.

yuca ~ (Cassava) A root that ranges from 6 to 12 inches long and 2 to 3 inches in diameter. Peeled, grated white flesh can be used to make cassareep (a West Indian condiment found in Caribbean markets) and tapioca.

zabaglione ~ A rich Italian custard made of egg yolks beaten with Marsala wine and sugar until very thick.

zest ~ The outer skin of citrus where the important oils have accumulated.

Recipe Index

Restaurant Index

Fine Dining Series

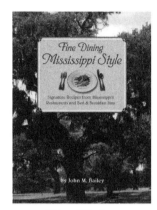   

**Fine Dining
Mississippi Style**

**Fine Dining
Louisiana Style**

**Fine Dining
Tennessee Style**

**Fine Dining
Georgia Style**

$\mathcal{W}$e hope that you have enjoyed *Fine Dining Georgia Style.*
Each book in the FINE DINING SERIES collects signature recipes from
the very best restaurants, chefs, and bed & breakfast inns in each
featured state.

Dedicated to Preserving America's Food Heritage for twenty-five
years, Quail Ridge Press is nationally renowned for the acclaimed
BEST OF THE BEST STATE COOKBOOK SERIES and RECIPE HALL OF
FAME COOKBOOK COLLECTION as well as the FINE DINING SERIES.

All of our cookbooks are available in bookstores, and gift and
kitchen shops nationwide. They can also be ordered directly from
Quail Ridge Press. To place an order or to request a free catalog,
call 1-800-343-1583 or visit us on the web at **www.quailridge.com**
where you'll also find special offers, free recipes, and more.

QUAIL RIDGE PRESS
Preserving America's Food Heritage

P. O. Box 123 • Brandon, MS 39043 • 1-800-343-1583 • www.quailridge.com